CU00409507

USS MISSOURI AT WAR

KIT & CAROLYN BONNER

ZENITH PRESS

To Carolyn E. Bonner: my wife, fellow naval historian,
and award-winning maritime photographer. There has been no one
better, and the field of naval history is better for her work.
—K.B.

First published in 2008 by Zenith Press, an imprint of
MBI Publishing Company, 400 1st Avenue North,
Suite 300, Minneapolis, MN 55401 USA.

© Kit and Carolyn Bonner, 2008

All rights reserved. With the exception of quoting brief
passages for the purposes of review, no part of this
publication may be reproduced without prior written
permission from the Publisher.

Zenith Press titles are also available at discounts in bulk
quantity for industrial or sales-promotional use. For
details write to Special Sales Manager at MBI Publishing
Company, 400 1st Avenue North, Suite 300, Minneapolis,
MN 55401 USA.

To find out more about our books, join us online at
www.zenithpress.com.

On the front cover: The USS *Missouri* fires several Mark 7
16-inch guns while underway off the coast of Hawaii,
July 1988. *U.S. Navy*
Inset: General Douglas MacArthur, supreme Allied
commander, sits at the surrender table and signs the
document with five pens. He is attended by Lt. Gen.
Jonathan Wainwright, U.S. Army, and British
Lt. Gen. Sir Archibald Percival. *U.S. Navy*

On the frontispiece: This spectacular view of the two
forward turrets of the *Missouri's* main battery, with the
USS *Arizona* Memorial just over the bow, was captured in
March 2006. *Author's collection*

On the title pages: The *Missouri* sits serenely at its
mooring along Battleship Row, long after being
refurbished. As a museum ship, there are none better,
and this particular view shows the great ship to its best
advantage. *USS* Missouri *Memorial Association*

On the back cover: The port side of the *Missouri's* bridge,
depicting all of the combat ribbons and stars for service
aboard. To the far right are symbols for ten Iraqi mines
that were destroyed by the ship's EOD team in the Persian
Gulf. The ship has now been repainted and looks almost
factory fresh. *U.S. Navy*

About the authors:
Kit Bonner and Carolyn Bonner are naval historians
and photographers. They have authored or co-authored
numerous books, including *USS Iowa at War, Modern
Warships, Great Ship Disasters, Warship Boneyards, Cold
War at Sea,* and *Great Naval Disasters.* Kit was the naval
consultant for the 1997 blockbuster film *Titanic.* The
Bonners live in Ione, California.

Library of Congress Cataloging-in-Publication Data

Bonner, Kit, 1945-
  USS Missouri at war / Kit and Carolyn Bonner.
    p. cm.
  ISBN 978-0-7603-3219-1 (pbk. : alk. paper) 1. Missouri
(Battleship : BB 63) I. Bonner, Carolyn. II. Title.
  VA65.M59B66 2008
  359.3'2520973—dc22
                                    2008012156

Editor: Steve Gansen
Designer: Danielle Smith

Printed in Singapore

CONTENTS

The battleship USS *Missouri* rests at its last mooring along Battleship Row in Pearl Harbor. Just forward of the *Missouri* is the *Arizona* Memorial, and together they make up an abstract set of bookends to the history of World War II in the Pacific. The battleship USS *Arizona* was destroyed by a surprise Japanese air attack on December 7, 1941, and the surrender of Imperial Japan was signed aboard the *Missouri* on September 3, 1945. *Author's collection*

CHAPTER ONE

HISTORY

IN EARLY 1960, MY FATHER WAS GIVEN HIS LAST assignment in the navy. He was told to report to the USS *Staten Island* (AGB-5) as the icebreaker's executive officer for a yearlong tour in the Arctic. Having just returned from duty in the Philippines, going from ninety degrees to minus-forty-five degrees was too much to ask. He asked for and was granted a different assignment as the personnel officer for the Pacific Reserve Fleet based in Bremerton, Washington.

The *Missouri* was the site of the Reserve Fleet's flagship and its headquarters for a time. My father's office was aboard the battleship very near the site of the surrender. After enough pleading, it was not long before I was allowed to haunt most of the ship. The *Missouri* was so big that exploring it at first required a twine tied to a starting point and my belt. Without this precaution, I might still be wandering through its compartments.

On the north side of the shipyard, a new navy was being built, or rebuilt, as the case was. The USS *Coral Sea* (CV-43) was just finishing a multi-year modernization, and the state-of-the-art missile frigates USS *Coontz* (DLG-9) and USS *King* (DLG-10) had undergone sea trials. What had been a big destroyer as recently as the Korean War (*Gearing* class at 390 feet in length) paled by comparison to the 512-foot-long frigates *Coontz* and *King,* which were 31 percent longer. Larger ships were now needed to house modern weapons, automation, and electronics that had come of age. Even massive dry docks were needed to accommodate the new supercarriers such as the *Constellation, Kitty Hawk,* and those planned to come.

The *Missouri* looms out of the fog at her mooring at the Inactive Ships Facility in Bremerton, Washington. She has remained at peace with the world for three decades in Bremerton, maintained by the navy against the day that she might again be called up. *U.S. Navy*

Aside from size, there was a hue and cry for missile-armed cruisers and destroyer-type ships. The gun had proven inadequate against the kamikazes (twenty-four thousand shells fired per aircraft downed), and the navy was convinced that the weapon to defeat the threat of guided missiles fired from future Soviet warships and high-speed aircraft (jets) was the long-range guided missile. Accordingly, new ships armed almost entirely with missile batteries were being constructed as well as cruiser conversions; three heavy cruisers (USS *Columbus* [CA-74], USS *Albany* [CA-123], and USS *Chicago* [CA-134]) were

being converted on a rush basis to mount Talos, Tartar, and ASROC systems. The only thought given the once-formidable gun battery carried was two open-mount, five-inch, .38-caliber weapons sited amidships. Someone had forgotten about small torpedo boats! The *Columbus* was being converted in the dock adjacent to the Reserve Fleet and would be designated CG-12 when completed on November 4, 1962. The missile was spelling the doom for many of the ships being preserved in mothballs.

Down at the south end of the shipyard was the Bremerton Group of the Pacific Reserve Fleet, and in

The *Missouri* and USS *New Jersey* sit at a pier that is open to the public in Bremerton. Nearly two thousand visitors per year trod the decks of the "Mighty Mo" looking for the surrender plaque embedded in the Burmese teakwood deck. *U.S. Navy*

A colorized version of HMS *Victory,* a huge ship of the line that carried over eight hundred personnel and was Adm. Horatio Nelson's flagship. Today, the *Victory* is enshrined in England as its most treasured naval artifact.

1960, the docks were crammed with World War II–and Korean War–era warships. There were so many silent ships that the inlet adjacent to the inactive ships had trots of older destroyers, light cruisers, antiaircraft cruisers, and even a few heavy cruisers. They were all awaiting the call to arms. It would come for very, very few to swell the fleet for the Vietnam Conflict and sustain the Cold War with the Soviet Union.

Ships such as the antiaircraft (AA) cruisers USS *Reno* (CL-96) and USS *San Diego* (CL-53) sat across from battleships USS *Alabama* (BB-60), USS *Maryland* (BB-45), and USS *West Virginia* (BB-48). The *Maryland* and *West Virginia* left for the scrap yard in late 1959. The antiaircraft cruisers left to be broken up within months of the other ships, and the auxiliary ships and small carriers left on a continuous

HMS *Dreadnought,* the first true battleship, was launched in 1906 for the Royal Navy. It was turbine powered and had multiple screws, and its main battery was of a single caliber. This precursor represented a quantum leap in technology to the future of heavy warship construction. *Author's collection*

basis. The ships that were destined to remain were the most modern, such as the *Iowa*-class battleships and *Essex*-class carriers.

As I lived in the shipyard on the hill overlooking the Reserve Fleet, weekends were filled with visits to ships and going through various dumpsters searching for artifacts, books, and such. I found six cruise books from the *Missouri* (1945 surrender issue) and several others, including those from the USS *Alabama,* USS *Reno,* and several auxiliaries (attack troop and cargo ships). I also got over my fear of small compartments by crawling around in these ships with a flashlight,

canteen filled with water, hard hat, and warm coat. I was careful never to take anything from the ships themselves. Little did I know that decades later, some ships would be archeological digs for naval historians who take pictures and, regrettably, thieves who would take anything.

However, there was one ship that stood out among all of the ships of all classes: the battleship USS *Missouri* (BB-63). She was modern, popular, and too valuable for scrapping, sale to a friendly power, or loan to another government agency. In short, the *Missouri* was and is a national landmark on the A-list

The German battle cruiser *Seydlitz* before the Battle of Jutland. The *Seydlitz* was very well built and could absorb a tremendous amount of punishment yet still keep fighting. During the Battle of Jutland, she was hit twenty-three times by heavy-caliber shells from the Royal Navy's battle line. Each battleship or battle cruiser built taught lessons on how to build the ultimate battleship. *Author's collection*

of national landmarks. This premier battleship was also a favorite with the Truman family, as it had been christened by Margaret Truman, daughter of President Harry S. Truman, a popular president who exuded all of the rough-hewn charm typical of Americans and their military machinery.

Just fifteen years before, the *Missouri* culminated its wartime service by being selected to hold the surrender ceremonies between the Allied powers and the Empire of Japan in Tokyo Bay. The date was September 2, 1945, and Imperial Japan was compelled to surrender by overwhelming military odds, including the American nuclear weapons. Japan unconditionally surrendered to the Allied Powers as led by Gen. Douglas MacArthur on the deck of the USS *Missouri*. As soon as the ink was dry on the rare parchment document, the news was flashed to an anxious world. A war that began on September 3, 1939, had finally drawn to a close. There was no armistice: it was complete capitulation and surrender, with no conditions accorded the defeated powers. The name of the *Missouri* was on the lips of people the world over. Shortly thereafter, the now famous battleship came home to the adulation of the American people.

Eventually, the celebrations died down, and amidst reductions in the fleet, the *Missouri* returned to service, however, on the other side of the world, in the Atlantic and Mediterranean. After helping to contain Communism in the eastern Mediterranean in 1946 and then doing a combat tour in Korea in 1952, the *Missouri* was placed in reserve in 1955 in Bremerton, Washington.

Interestingly, when the *Missouri* was berthed close to the highway running into the City of Bremerton, the navy allowed visitors on some of the exterior decks and around the surrender plaque. For nearly thirty years, the aging battleship was a must-see tourist attraction averaging 180,000 visitors annually. Ironically, many of the modern warships of the mid-1950s that were needed for national defense now shared space in the "boneyard" with the *Missouri.*

THE MISSOURI AND ITS CONTEMPORARIES

No introduction to a book about the USS *Missouri* would be complete without reference to the popular ship's contemporaries around the world. During the late nineteenth century up through the mid-twentieth

This plaque covers the location onboard the *Missouri* where the actual surrender document was signed by all of the warring parties. The paper upon which the wording was placed was an ancient parchment located in the basement of a monastery in Manila, Territory of the Philippines. The *Missouri* was at anchor in Tokyo Bay during the signing. *U.S. Navy*

After the final refit of the *Missouri* in the 1980s, she proudly steams beneath the Golden Gate Bridge. Of all of the ships in the U.S. Navy, none are more aesthetically beautiful than the brute-like strength of the *Missouri* and sister ships of the *Iowa* class. *U.S. Navy*

century, nearly every nation with a credible navy employed battleships. Italy, France, Germany, England, the United States, Japan, and the Soviet Union were the primary owners and operators of dreadnoughts. Speed, armor, armament, and displacement were criteria used to determine the most powerful of these ships. Certain South American navies contracted with various European shipyards for their own battleships.

The real apex of capital-ship growth was during the early twentieth century, when there was a wholesale expansion of battleships among nations desiring a place at the naval-power table. The battleship was the gauge of a nation's prosperity and willingness to protect its interests at sea. One of England's earliest leaders once stated that "it is upon the navy under the good providence of God that the wealth, safety,

and strength of the King do chiefly depend." He was reflecting the same belief that every government leader later subscribed to, including George Washington, who recognized that the fledgling United States would be defenseless without a credible and modern navy. Washington was cautioning the nation, which had just sold off its last ship, the 440-ton *Alfred.*

As trade widened from border to border and continent to continent, naval protection became crucial against pirates, privateers, and other navies that sought to intercept and capture shipments. Yet, piracy was minor compared to one-upmanship among nations. The battleship was the "arm" in the arms race during this period, and so much so that artificial limitations were worked out among the primary nations.

The USS *Iowa* (BB-61) participating in Ocean Safari '85 on September 1, 1985. This was one of the innumerable exercises that these ships were involved in. *U.S. Navy*

From 1860 to 1960, the era of the armored battleship reigned supreme. Before that, Great Britain's Royal Navy dominated the seas with its massive, heavy-gun, wooden ships of the line. The rules changed with the introduction of steam power, the screw or propeller drive, breechloading weapons that could be trained, and steel construction or substantial armor plate. The day of sail power, ponderous wooden hulls, and hundreds of men simply to operate miles of running rigging was quickly passing into history. By the late 1800s, sail-powered ships of the line with around one hundred heavy cannons, such as Vice Admiral Nelson's HMS *Victory,* had become ceremonial platforms. To this day, the "First-Rater" *Victory* is immobilized in dry dock and the flagship of the second sea lord. It is also the oldest commissioned ship in the world. However, it is light years behind the battleships developed during the heyday of these huge and near-mythical warships.

The period when the battleship reached its zenith of power, importance, and respectability was in the years between World War I and World War II. Of course, many refinements had taken place before this period with the introduction of the HMS *Dreadnought,* the all-big-gun (single-caliber), turbine-drive, quadruple-screw battleship of 1906. This ship led the way to the modern battleship as no other had or would. The arrangement of its main battery ensured that eight 12-inch guns could be brought to bear on a target, and the turbine drive, which was also a novelty, could drive the 18,187-ton ship through the water at 21.6 knots.

The USS *New Jersey* (BB-62) was reactivated for a short period during the Vietnam War. Her long-range 16-inch guns had a very telling effect on the Vietcong and the operations of the North Vietnamese government. Most of the villages and industrial capabilities of the north were within a very few miles of the seaboard. *U.S. Navy*

Germany reciprocated with a number of battleships and battle cruisers, including the battle cruiser *Seydlitz*. She fought at the Battle of Jutland when the High Seas Fleet met the Grand Fleet in what was to be the all-inclusive gun duel, beginning on May 31, 1916. The *Seydlitz* was struck twenty-three times by heavy-caliber projectiles. Despite taking on a precarious amount of seawater, the ship was saved. This ship taught future designers the lesson of effective damage control and compartmentalization in battleship construction.

Of course, the popular heavy warship HMS *Hood* and its nemesis, the German navy's *Bismarck,* dominated the news in the summer of 1941. The most serious threat to the Allied lifeline was the destructive power of the super battleships *Bismarck, Tirpitz,* and

the other heavy ships in the German surface fleet. There were few ships in the Royal Navy that could defeat the *Bismarck* or *Tirpitz* at sea, and once loose in the convoy lanes, it was possible to really disrupt the supply lines to England and the Soviet Union from the west.

In late May 1941, the opportunity presented itself for the Royal Navy to destroy the *Bismarck*. The 42,370-ton battleship mounting eight 15-inch guns sortied with the heavy cruiser *Prinz Eugen* on May 18. The actual plan was for the battleships *Scharnhorst* and *Gneisenau* to sail in tandem, and then this formidable force would attack the Allied convoys. The two latter ships were unable to sail, and the *Bismarck* and *Prinz Eugen* were soon sighted by a Spitfire flying reconnaissance.

The USS *Wisconsin* (BB-64) after its 1985 refit with Tomahawk, Harpoon, and close-in weapons systems. When the *Iowa* class was first built, they were the finest battleships in the world. With the electronic, automation, and weapons upgrades, they became the most powerful battleships ever to grace the seas. *U.S. Navy*

The starboard side of the USS *Missouri* as a memorial ship and museum. The small barred *V* forward on the hull at the waterline gives the identity away as an inactive vessel. This is a flooding mark to warn caretakers about the condition of the ship's watertight integrity. This image shows the *Missouri* to good effect, and she is as tight as a drum. *U.S. Navy*

The Royal Navy's Home Fleet sortied the *Hood* and *Prince of Wales* accompanied by six destroyers, which, combined, were considered capable of sweeping the seas of the German ships. A short but epic battle took place on May 24 at daybreak. Incredibly, through a series of events, the *Hood* was struck by shells from both her opponents and suddenly disintegrated in a cataclysmic explosion, leaving only three survivors. The *Prince of Wales* was also mauled before leaving the area.

The *Hood* was lost due to a lack of sufficient armor over critical areas, and the plunging fire of the *Bismarck* and *Prinz Eugen* found this weakness and exploited it. The philosophy that "speed is armor" was a design corollary for battle cruisers such as the *Hood*, and this was proven wrong when heavily armored and armed battleships matched the speed of the battle cruiser.

Within days, elements of the Royal Navy ran the *Bismarck* to earth and sank her with a combination of aerial and ship-launched torpedoes and heavy gunfire from at least two battleships.

There were few battleship-versus-battleship duels during World War II, and the *Hood* versus the *Bismarck* was the most famous and revealing. War at sea now required a variety of warship types, and it would be quite rare for a repeat of that battle. The few clashes between capital ships during the war years were anticlimactic compared to the events in the summer of 1941. Of course, the grandfathers of all battleships were the twin 71,659-ton behemoths completed by Japan on the eve of the Pacific war, the IJN *Mushashi*

506 — La " Bretagne " Ecole des Mousses.

A. Bougault

The French ship of the line or battleship of 1850, *La Bretagne,* with several boats slung out. *La Bretagne* was unknowingly obsolete at birth, and would be even more so in 1862, when the USS *Monitor* made its appearance during the American Civil War. This ship was multi-deck and mounted ninety guns per side. She displaced 5,100 tons on 234 feet in length, and crew conditions must have been abhorrent due to space constraints. *Author's collection*

This is Turner's celebrated painting, *The Fighting Temeraire,* showing the ship under tow by a sidewheel tugboat. Joseph Mallord William Turner captured the spirit of the end of an era as steam pulled sail to its final resting place in this 1838 work. The ship of the line *Temeraire* was no longer of value to the Royal Navy with the advent of steam, steel plating, rifled guns that were breechloading, and a number of other modernisms. *Treasure Island Museum*

and IJN *Yamato.* These battleships mounted nine 18.1-inch guns in their main battery and twelve 6-inch guns in their secondary. Both were dispatched by a combination of bombs and aerial torpedoes from Allied aircraft carriers late in the war.

Yet, navies continued to build battleships throughout World War II; however, they were used for vastly different tasks. Great Britain holds the honor for the last battleship built: the 44,500-ton HMS *Vanguard.* This 814-foot-long ship mounted eight 15-inch guns and was commissioned in April 1946.

THE USS MISSOURI: A SHIP OF DESTINY

The *Missouri* was the last of ten battleships completed in the early 1940s, and the last battleship commissioned in the U.S. Navy. From the earliest—the USS *Washington* (BB-56) and USS *North Carolina*

(BB-55)—to the last—the USS *Wisconsin* (BB-64) and finally the USS *Missouri* (BB-63)—each had a special nickname, accomplishment, or something rare and unusual that set it apart from all of the others. Circumstances, the crew, or simply the lore of the sea often chooses a ship as being a cut above others and destined for great achievements. Apparently, the word spread throughout the navy that the USS *Missouri* was likely to fall into this category.

For decades, the American public had placed its faith in its battleships, and after the devastation of Pearl Harbor, the nation needed to see the familiar battle line as a sign that the U.S. Navy was only down and not beaten. The aircraft carrier was actually the power of this war, but to the average citizen on the day after the Japanese attacked Pearl Harbor, the carrier played second fiddle to the old, dependable battleship. As long as the navy had modern battleships, no nation

A panoramic view of the Battle of Hampton Roads on March 9, 1862. The USS *Monitor* is fiercely shooting at the CSS *Virginia,* which has been driven away from the USS *Minnesota.* The *Minnesota* appears to be sinking by the stern and is afire forward, but the fire was minor and lasted just a few minutes. It seems as if every weapon in Chesapeake Bay is firing at something, so the painting is not the most accurate rendition of the action that took place. It does, however, depict the massive changing of the guard from wood and sail to iron and steam. *Treasure Island Museum*

on earth could defeat the United States. Besides, the general public was unaware of the time lapse from design to commissioning of one of these steel monsters. The *Missouri* was commissioned in the next to the last year of the Pacific War, on January 29, 1944. The actual design began in the 1930s.

There was something almost mythically special about the *Missouri* in that she was considered to be an exceptional ship that was blessed with a crucial destiny. No one knew what the destiny consisted of, yet for thousands of enlistees and current officers and ratings, the *Missouri* was the ship to be assigned to. Over three thousand commissioned officers in the navy applied for transfer to the new battleship during its pre-commissioning period. Just a partial list of those advantages that attracted the best personnel to the *Missouri* was:

- Construction that was far superior to any other battleship in the world

- Nine 16-inch guns, each of which could throw the equivalent of a 1940 Ford over twenty-four miles
- Bunks with mattresses rather than the back-breaking hammock
- A bakery that could produce 1,800 loaves of fresh bread daily
- The ability to produce one thousand quarts of ice cream per day for its soda fountains and general mess
- A laundry that could clean, press, and wrap clothing for 2,500 men each day
- A 212,000 shaft-horsepower (SHP) powerplant could train the three giant two–thousand–ton turrets with three 16-inch barrels with ease, and power hundreds of secondary motors and the main propulsion system
- A black gang (engineering staff) the size of two full destroyer crews (five hundred men) to keep all systems on line
- First televised launching of a warship

On June 11, 1944, the ship was commissioned, and one of the honored guests was Senator Harry S. Truman, among others. He wanted to make certain that the ship representing his state got a proper sendoff. It would not be long before Senator Truman and the USS *Missouri* would be intertwined in world history.

The battleship did not disappoint those who moved heaven and earth to be assigned to its crew. She fought in the Pacific Theater of World War II, and in the end, played host to the surrender signing in Tokyo Bay. This event formally ended the most violent war that mankind has ever engaged in, and on the decks of the *Missouri*, the Allied nations came to honor peace and receive the homage of the Pacific aggressor, Japan.

She was called upon to beat back Communism in the Eastern Mediterranean and Korea, and in 1955,

placed in reserve in Bremerton, Washington. There she sat for year after year and decade after decade.

In the mid-1980s, after three decades in mothballs, the *Missouri* again came alive, but now as a 1930s-designed battleship rearmed with microchips, automation, and a variety of missiles and new weapons. Its next task, along with fellow *Iowa* class battleships, was to checkmate Soviet ambitions at sea, and in some instances combat growing unrest and violence in the Mid-East. This final period of active combat came to an end with Gulf War I, when the forces of Iraq were ejected from Kuwait in 1991.

The *Missouri* and the U.S. Navy's other battleships were again retired, likely for the final time, in the early 1990s. Each of the four *Iowa*-class battleships found a home or is in the process of being placed as a memorial. The USS *Iowa* (BB-61) is on the U.S. Navy's

The USS *Texas* was known as a prototype battleship, or a second-class battleship and, later, a coastal battleship. There was the USS *Maine* and the *Texas,* which were the U.S. Navy's first effort at designing and building a battleship. The *Texas* was 301 feet in length, with a 64-foot beam and displaced 6,315 tons. Its maximum armor thickness was 12 inches, and it mounted an eclectic gun battery of two 12-inch, .35-caliber weapons; two 6-inch, .40-caliber guns (all breechloading); plus a variety of smaller, quick-firing guns. In addition, there were four torpedo tubes that fired 18-inch Whitehead torpedoes. The *Texas*'s performance was based on vertical-triple-expansion (VTE) engines that generated 8,610 horsepower and up to 17.8 knots. She was commissioned on August 15, 1895. Her sister, the USS *Maine,* was sunk in Havana Harbor on February 15, 1898. *Author's collection*

donation-hold list in California; the USS *New Jersey* (BB-62) has been donated to Camden, New Jersey; and the USS *Wisconsin* (BB-64) proudly sits adjacent to the Nauticus Museum in Norfolk, Virginia. As for the *Missouri,* in 1996 the ship was donated to a group in Pearl Harbor, and on June 22, 1998, amidst thousands of cheering onlookers, the well-worn and deserving ship arrived at its new and final berth along Battleship Row. The *Missouri's* bow is pointed away from the main channel, unlike its pre–World War II predecessors, which might have needed to get to sea quickly in times of emergency.

SEVEN HUNDRED YEARS OF BATTLESHIPS

In Asia as well as the European continent, the battleship had its origins over seven hundred years ago. The Chinese first employed junks which had towers located bow and stern that could house fighting men with crude weapons. As the years progressed and warlords saw the benefits of larger and larger ships, the junks became huge fighting machines at sea. Gunpowder, rockets, and other explosive weapons were also introduced, and the secrets of the East gradually made their way to the West.

At the same time, the European seafaring nations recognized that navies were imperative to guard and protect trade. In the years between 1300 and 1400 A.D., a ship type dubbed the "cog" was developed, which was a merchant ship with castle-like structures at either end. These housed bowmen and spear throwers to ward off enemies, including pirates and the dreaded Vikings or Norsemen. Nothing struck greater fear in the hearts of English or Irish fishermen or farmers than the cry, "Norsemen or Vikings." The bearded men from the north were superb seamen and violent beyond words with their axes, broadswords, and other hand weapons. It seemed as if they had no mercy, and that was half of their lore. They would sweep into an area in longboats crowded with armed men who foraged for their food, ale, and women. From the beginning of the Viking threat until it ended, there were 347 raids on English soil.

The best method for engaging these raiders was at sea. They sailed in open rowing craft assisted by single sails. They could be defeated by modern armed ships. The cog was an even match for them; it just took good ship handling and courage to face the enemy.

For nearly two centuries, England, France, and other European nations who were actively engaged in sea trade made increasing use of the cogs. If Europe was to emerge from the dark ages, merchant shipping had to expand and be protected. Seven hundred years later and in the early twenty-first century off the Somalia coast of Africa, the same is still true. Raiders in small launches range far and wide from the coast of Somalia to snatch merchant and passenger ships. All that has changed is the ship types and the weapons; the motivation is no different. The role and objectives are still the same and have been throughout the history of men who fight at sea.

As the 1400s waned, a new type of ship began to appear: the carrack. These were better sailing craft and could fire a broadside into its enemies. The English warship *Mary Rose* (1546) was a prime example of a carrack. It carried a broadside of thirty-nine cannons per side and displaced five hundred tons, with a length of 165 feet. By 1500, the popular galleon had appeared in almost all European navies, and this type of ship changed naval warfare dramatically. It was larger still than the carrack and far more maneuverable. But, the primary advantage was in numbers that could form a line of battle and fire broadside after broadside into its enemy. The age of hand-to-hand fighting at sea was vanishing, to be replaced by gun duels similar to those that occurred centuries later at Jutland and Leyte Gulf, where huge ships loosed heavy gunfire until one was driven from battle or sunk. The castles at either end of the galleons grew higher and higher, to allow the gunners to fire down into the opposing vessels. However, there was a point of diminishing returns, as the castles proved to be the downfall of the galleon—they interfered with the sailing qualities of the ship. Ships became wholly dependent on wind when the galley, which was primarily driven by oar power, fell into disuse.

The galleon gave way to a variety of ships based on their numbers of decks and guns, with as many as 144 guns on one vessel. The ship of the line was an English invention. The Royal Navy established a six-ship rating system dependent on the number of guns. The most popular was the seventy-four-gun ship of the line, or "74," although there were ships such as the French *Valmy* (1847) that sported three huge decks with flat, right-angle sides. It was one of the last, huge, all-sail three-deckers, with well over one

The USS *Indiana* (BB-1), the U.S. Navy's first battleship or pre-dreadnought. The *Indiana* is steaming at slow speed with just a whiff of coal smoke coming from its number two funnel. Its sisters were the USS *Massachusetts* (BB-2) and the USS *Oregon* (BB-3). The *Indiana* class was 348 feet in length and displaced 10,288 tons. Its maximum armor thickness (on the turret facing) was eighteen inches. The class was armed with four 13-inch, .35-caliber guns; eight 8-inch, .35-caliber guns; and a variety of other weapons. It had a VTE engine that developed 9,738 horsepower for a top speed on two screws of 15.55 knots. The *Indiana* was disposed of as a bombing target after World War I on November 1, 1920. *Author's collection*

hundred cannon. At best it was unstable, much like the Swedish warship *Vasa*, which sank due to faulty engineering shortly after being launched. Collectively, these new multi-deck ships or battleships were known as "ships of the line." Later in the nineteenth century, they became known as the "main line of battle ship," which ultimately became "battleship."

Steam was making its appearance as a propulsion form, and this too was making changes in the type and design of the ship of the line. In fact, the ship of

the line that was solely powered by sail was obsolete by the mid-1800s. The French did build purpose-built battleships of the *Le Napoleon* class in 1850 that depended on a combination of steam and sail. One of the nine ships in the class was the *La Bretagne*, which displaced 5,100 tons, was 234 feet in length, and mounted ninety guns on five decks. Its top speed was 12.1 knots, and it had an endurance of forty days at sea. It was powered by a screw as opposed to paddle wheels. The last of this class was built in 1860, and like

Three views of the early twentieth century's revolutionary battleship, the HMS *Dreadnought*. The brainchild of British designers, it took advantage of many new concepts. All heavy guns were of the same caliber, and the ship was powered by a turbine, thus giving it greater speed. By the time the *Dreadnought* took to the water, all nations with substantial navies wanted a dreadnought, and anything else was obsolete. *Treasure Island Museum*

all sail warships, all wood warships, or even partial sail and steam warships, their day had come and gone. Even Lord Nelson's flagship HMS *Victory* had become wholly obsolete and was destined to become a museum ship.

The death of 550 years of warship development was due to a battle in the American Civil War in Hampton Roads in the Chesapeake Bay. It was March 8 and 9, 1862, and the Federal Navy chose to blockade the Confederate States from shipping or receiving any foreign goods. The idea was to strangle the Southern states in terms of weapons, supplies, medicine, and food. The plan was working; however, the South had decided to take the captured hull of the former Union steam sloop (USS *Merrimack*) and turn it into an ironclad. Over a period of a year, the newly christened CSS *Virginia* was heavily armed and heavily

armored, and after being completed, it steamed down to Hampton Roads to destroy the Union blockading force of wooden warships. On March 8, the rather strange-looking craft slowly steamed toward its quarry, and by the end of the day, had nearly destroyed the hope of the Union Navy in preserving the blockade. The USS *Cumberland* was sunk, as was the USS *Congress.* The USS *Minnesota* ran aground, and *Virginia* could not get in close enough to destroy this last major vessel. The damage had been done to the Union pride in front of the international media and observers from navies from all over the world. Many waited with bated breath for what would be a complete victory by the Confederacy over the Union blockading squadron. Unknown to many, the USS *Monitor,* the Union Navy's answer to the Confederate ironclad, had arrived just after midnight on March 9, 1862, and was hidden behind the *Minnesota.* Lieutenant John Worden, the commanding officer of the *Monitor,* had his orders: protect the USS *Minnesota* and the blockading fleet and defeat whatever the Confederacy sent down the river.

The following morning, the *Virginia* was greeted by what appeared to be a raft with a cheese box on it. There was much jeering and laughter until the little ship opened fire. It was Swedish inventor John Ericsson's *Monitor,* more than an even match for an armored ship.

Despite every attempt made by the *Virginia* to destroy the *Minnesota,* the *Monitor,* with its revolving turret, nine inches of armor, and two 11-inch Dahlgren smoothbore guns, stood in the way. After four hours of trading punches, the leaking *Virginia* steamed up the Elizabeth River and never again engaged the *Monitor.* The blockade was still in effect, and the *Monitor* had just a few dents.

In actuality, the *Monitor* was the true precursor to the USS *Missouri* and all of the twentieth century's modern battleships. It also led the way to many inventions that made submersibles possible.

THE REIGN OF STEAM, IRON, STEEL, AND RIFLED GUNS BEGINS

The *Monitor* came out of the Battle of Hampton Roads as the definite favorite among naval enthusiasts, naval officers worldwide, and the media. By the end of the day on March 9, 1862, naval warfare had gone through a metamorphosis. No longer could a wooden ship powered by the capricious mannerisms of wind hope to defeat an armored, steam-propelled warship. This was especially true when a screw and turrets were employed, giving the iron ship an even greater advantage.

There were those who could not let go of the past, and consequently, the navies of the world let them go. The evidence at Hampton Roads was too compelling, and this was just the beginning. Advances would take place rapidly, and those nations that embraced new technology and cast aside old-fashioned ideas would then have the most powerful navies.

As the American Civil War progressed, Ericsson's monitors became larger and more sophisticated with two and even three turrets. However, the monitors had difficulty with overall seaworthiness because the freeboard was less than twenty inches, and in

anything other than a mill pond, the ships could possibly founder. In point of fact, the original *Monitor* did founder on December 31, 1862, when she was swamped off Cape Hatteras. The ship was under tow at the time, and sixteen of her sixty-two-man crew perished. Aside from the likelihood that a seaway would swamp a monitor, there were problems with loading the guns and aiming the turret at the target in a timely manner. During the famous battle, the guns had to be retracted and muzzle fed before re-aiming and firing. This hampered rapid firing and endangered the gun crew from enemy shrapnel. In 1865, the American Civil War ended with a Union victory and reunification of the United States. Regrettably little real progress was made in remedying the problems identified with the monitors and ironclads in general. Old admirals, commodores, and captains again ruled the U.S. Navy and saw no purpose in continued development of modern battleships. After all, it was three thousand miles from the nearest potential enemy. The United States was again looking inward and westward; there was no need for an oceangoing navy.

Union generals now ruled the military and had little use for a merchant fleet or warships to guard them or the nation. Even American ships sent to represent the navy were old sailing vessels, and all of the advances made during the Civil War seem to have been forgotten. It was so absurd that ships could only run on coal during emergencies and had to rely on sail for primary power. It was this way and worse until the 1880s. The navy had dropped from great respectability to a twelfth-rate force. China and Chile exceeded the American navy in the number and quality of its ironclads. Finally, the navy began to rebuild what was known as the ABCD ships, or the modern ironclads: USS *Atlanta,* USS *Baltimore,* USS *Chicago,* and USS *Dolphin.* With the exception of the *Dolphin,* the others were rated as cruisers with a mix of 8-inch, 6-inch, and 4-inch weapons and with speeds in excess of 15 knots. The armor was minimal at 1.5 inches, but it was a beginning. Construction of the battleships came in 1895 and continued until the end of World War II.

Next came the USS *Texas* and USS *Maine,* which were dubbed prototypes to the battleships. As the *Texas* was commissioned first on August 15, 1895, less than four weeks before the *Maine,* she is considered the first battleship in some quarters. In reality, the first-rated pre-dreadnought battleship was the USS *Indiana* (BB-1). It was characterized by the following:

- Coastal defense battleship responsible for littoral protection of the United States
- 348 feet in length, with a 69-foot beam, and displaced 10,288 tons
- Armament consisting of four 13-inch, .35-caliber breechloading rifles; eight 8-inch, .35-caliber breechloaders; four 6-inch, .40-caliber breechloading rifles, and a host of smaller quick-firing weapons
- Armor of 18 inches per side and 15 inches on the turrets
- Twin-screw, vertical-triple-expansion (VTE) propulsion (coal), 9,738 horsepower, for 15.55 knots full speed

The USS *Massachusetts* (BB-2) and USS *Oregon* (BB-3) were sister battleships.

The first non-coastal battleships were the six-ship *Connecticut* class. At 450 feet in length and displacing sixteen thousand tons, these ships were armed with a mix of 12-inch, 8-inch, 7-inch, and 3-inch guns. The armor was 11 inches, and the maximum speed on 16,500 horsepower was 18.78 knots.

Of course, Great Britain, France, Italy, and Russia were rearming with modern warships, as was Japan in the Far East. The ocean served as a moat around the United States, and it was this way until 1898. Then, the United States went to war with Spain. A weaker opponent on the European continent could not have been chosen. American warships easily defeated the Spanish fleet in Manila Bay and later in Cuban waters. Spain had ignored its navy for too many years, and like its neighbor far to the north, Czarist Russia, it depended on its history and reputation as an Old-World European power. Commodore Dewey's shells literally tore the Spanish fleet to pieces in Manila Bay, and the same result occurred off Cuba. Just a few years later, the Japanese soundly defeated the Russian Navy at the Battle of Tsushima on May 27, 1905. The Russian Squadron was trained, and other of the Czar's armed forces were likewise forced to capitulate due to inattention to modern equipment, inadequate leadership, a rotting government, and poor morale aboard its ships.

Of course, the U.S. Navy also needed much improvement; however, there was time and excellent leadership available. One such leader was Lt. William S. Sims, who wrote directly to President Theodore Roosevelt about the appalling gunnery scores at the Naval Battle of Santiago. Of a total of eight thousand shells fired, an incredibly poor 123 hits were registered. The navy had done no better at Manila Bay, with a 4 percent hit rate. For a junior officer to complain directly to the president was unheard of, yet Sims was passionate about accurate gunnery and the defense of the United States. Another was Lt. Comdr. Albert P. Niblack, who was also ashamed of the fleet's record. Roosevelt concurred and allowed the "young Turks" to have their opinion. It proved to be a profitable decision for the navy. Within months, and after studying the Royal Navy's method, the fleet had witnessed substantial leaps and bounds in improvement. The solution was simple: centralized gunfire control. All guns miss, or all gun hit the target! Younger officers began taking an active interest in modern gunnery and engineering, and not just how to fit their uniforms and behave at an admiral's tea party.

All modern navies had moved from sail power and wooden construction to steam and iron or steel. The U.S. Navy was no different, except that it had a tendency to be a half-step behind the rest of the international naval community. Defeating the Spanish navy was no feat of arms, as most of Spain's navy was rotting at its moorings and far behind the times. Of course, President Theodore Roosevelt was anxious to have a cutting-edge navy, but in 1906, the Royal Navy stole a march on all other navies with HMS *Dreadnought*. The popular saying was, "Dread Nought but God!" Ironically, the U.S. Navy had designed battleships with all-centerline, superfiring turrets (turrets set back and above a main deck turret to provide the ship with maximum firepower) of uniform, large-caliber guns. These were the *Michigan* (BB-27) and *South Carolina* (BB-26), which were designed before the *Dreadnought*, yet did not enter fleet service until 1910, four years after HMS *Dreadnought*. In a world where the important thing is when a ship is actually in the water and operational, the date of its design is somewhat of a moot point. The *Dreadnought* took to the sea in

1906, and the *Michigan* and *South Carolina,* four years later, were post-dreadnoughts, of which there were twenty-nine ships.

Just as the U.S. Navy had adapted to all-steel ships, heavy-caliber breechloading rifled weapons, redundant armor protection, and steam-propelled battleships, the HMS *Dreadnought* and ultimately thirty-one follow-on ships over the next seven years stunned the naval world. By 1913, the Royal Navy had dreadnought-type battleships that were sequentially being upgraded and improved. The U.S. Navy's *Michigan* and *South Carolina* were improved with superfiring guns that became standard on all modern capital ships.

The early-twentieth-century precursor of the USS *Missouri* (BB-63) was the USS *Missouri* (BB-11), a member of the *Maine* class of coastal battleships, built in 1902 as a successor to the USS *Maine* of Spanish-American War fame. This 13,500-ton-full-load ship was commissioned on December 11, 1903, and was 394 feet in length, with a crew of 561 officers and enlisted men. She was armed with a main battery of four 12-inch, .45-caliber guns and sixteen 6-inch, .50-caliber weapons. Her secondary battery was made of six 3-inch, .50-caliber guns and smaller, quick-firing weapons. Her speed was eighteen knots on sixteen thousand horsepower. Providing propulsion were coal-fired reciprocating engines and two screws. She was finally broken up as the result of the Washington Naval Arms Limitation Treaty of February 8, 1922. *U.S. Navy*

The USS *Michigan* (BB-27), an American-designed dreadnought, predated HMS *Dreadnought* by at least two years. The *Michigan* and sister, USS *South Carolina* (BB-26), were not actually commissioned until 1910, thus making HMS *Dreadnought* the hands-down winner in the "dreadnought race." The *South Carolina* and *Michigan* set the stage for another innovative design feature, the superfiring guns of the main battery fore and aft. The wing-mounted main battery was now obsolete. In the race to develop the most powerful weapons, navies employed any advantage, and then competing nations copied it. Soon, the superfiring main battery would become standard. *Treasure Island Museum*

CHAPTER TWO

WORLD WAR I AND INTERWAR YEARS

IN AUGUST 1914, WORLD WAR CONSUMED Europe, and it was primarily a land war that raged over the continent. However, there were at least two major confrontations between Germany and England at sea: the Battle of Dogger Bank and, of course, the most prominent, the Battle of Jutland, which took place May 31–June 1, 1916. The combatants were the Grand Fleet of England and the German High Seas Fleet, and the battle was fought in the North Sea near the Jutland Peninsula of Denmark. The Royal Navy was commanded by Sir John Jellicoe and Sir David Beatty, who had 151 ships at their disposal, including 28 battleships, 9 battlecruisers, and 112 heavy and light cruisers plus destroyers.

The High Seas Fleet was commanded by Adm. Reinhard Scheer and Adm. Franz von Hipper, and at their command were 102 ships, which were primarily light forces, including 61 torpedo boats. However, they did have 16 battleships, 5 battlecruisers, 6 pre-dreadnoughts, and 11 light cruisers. What the German navy lacked in numbers, it made up for in the quality of their warships.

Jutland was to be the ultimate testing ground for all of the advancements in the development of the battleship and naval tactics in general. Amazingly, certain facts came out that surprised both belligerents. German warships were apt to survive even the worst pummeling, because they were more heavily armored

The USS *Texas* (BB-35), a dreadnought, is still in existence as a memorial battleship at the San Jacinto Battleground State Historical Site in Texas. A visit to this ship truly shows how sailors lived, from ten-holer toilet facilities to hammocks that had to be slung in the gunroom of the secondary battery of 5-inch, .51-caliber casemate guns, and, ultimately, food preparation aft in the open so as not to risk fire from massive, oil-fired ranges. *Author's collection*

The German High Seas Fleet battle cruiser SMS *Seydlitz* absorbed 23 major hits at the Battle of Jutland but was able to limp back to Germany. Superior damage control plus compartmentalization saved the ship from foundering or exploding when a critical area was struck. This was not true of the British battle cruisers, which seemed to go up like a Roman candle when hit in the wrong place. *Author's collection*

and compartmentalized compared to the ships of the Royal Navy. The Germans preferred armor over armament, and this preference paid dividends. One of their battleships, the SMS *Seydlitz,* was hit 23 times by large and moderate-size shells and a torpedo. Due to its construction with interlocking compartmentalization and attention to damage control, the *Seydlitz* successfully limped back to port carrying over one thousand tons of excess seawater. The same could not be said for the severely damaged ships of the Royal Navy. The fact that the British warships did not protect their powder and shell magazines was borne out by battle cruisers that literally exploded, jackknifed, and sank with all but a small number of their crew.

In summary, the German fleet that came out to break the British blockade nearly did so against horrendous odds. They might have prevailed if they had more battleships available. As it was, the Royal Navy lost 6,094 killed and fourteen warships, whereas the German navy suffered the loss of 2,551 men and eleven warships. Neither lost a battleship, but together they lost four battle cruisers. This was a major lesson. A lightly armored warship has no business in the battle line during a slugging match. The battle cruiser needed space to achieve its high speed to avoid enemy fire, and this was impossible if it was constrained in the battle line. The ship type was badly used, and later in history, could not stand up to battleships, as in the case of HMS *Hood* versus SMS *Bismarck*, or aircraft,

HMS *Hood* was the pride of the Royal Navy, upon which the empire pinned its hopes. It was a devastating blow to British pride when the *Bismarck* dispatched the *Hood* with a few salvoes and left a mere three survivors floating on the surface. It fell to the cloth and metal tubing biplanes (Swordfish, or "String Bags") to slow the *Bismarck* down with torpedo hits so that the Home Fleet could finish her with its heavy guns and torpedoes. *Author's collection*

as witnessed HMS *Prince of Wales* and HMS *Repulse* versus Japanese bombers and torpedo planes shortly after the attack on Pearl Harbor.

The clash of the titans at Jutland will be analyzed and discussed for years to come. In essence, neither side was a winner, nor did either party take any real note of the lessons taught by that conflict.

THE UNITED STATES JOINS THE FIGHT

The United States did not enter the war until 1917, but at the same time, it was rebuilding its fleet based on a solid 1916 appropriation by Congress that provided for scores of destroyers, cruisers, and various classes of battleship. Incredibly, the navy built a total of eleven separate classes of battleship before arriving at the

Imperial Japanese Navy *Nagato* was the first battleship in the world to be armed with 16-inch (actually 16.1-inch) guns in the main battery. When built, this ship was also the fastest battleship in any navy, at 26.7 knots in 1920. The *Nagato* figured prominently throughout World War II and relayed the message to attack Pearl Harbor to the carrier attack force in 1941. In 1946, the old battleship was disposed of in the nuclear blasts at Bikini Atoll during Operation Crossroads. *Treasure Island Museum*

The French navy was also a major competitor in the naval arms race of the early twentieth century. The *Richelieu* as well as the *Jean Bart* and two unfinished battleships were built to checkmate the Italian navy's battleships. The *Richelieu* was commissioned during the spring of 1940 on the eve of France's surrender to the Germans. The *Richelieu* displaced 47,548 tons full load, and was 247.9 meters in length. She could make 30 knots on 150,000 horsepower and was powered by four geared turbines. Armament consisted of eight 15-inch guns with a secondary battery of nine 6-inch weapons plus a large number of antiaircraft guns. The *Richelieu* did not remain part of Vichy, and became part of the Free French movement. *Author's collection*

Iowa class in the early 1940s. These were not coastal battleships, but were oceangoing, blue-water fighting ships. Of course, Great Britain, Germany, France, Italy, and Japan were also building first-rate modern battleships. Some of these, including those built by the U.S. Navy, would fight not only in World War I but, after improvements, could be seen in World War II.

Beginning in 1911, the U.S. Navy commissioned two battleships, the USS *Florida* and USS *Utah*. Both had a main battery of 12-inch, .45-caliber guns and were ponderous ships that could go no faster than 20 knots. This was to be true for eight of the separate classes built from 1911 to 1921, although some of the later ships could make up to 23 knots.

The Imperial Japanese Navy *Yamato* was armed with nine 18.1-inch guns, the largest of any ship in the world. Of the three ships laid down as part of the *Yamato* class, only two were completed as battleships: IJN *Yamato* and IJN *Musashi*. The third was finished an aircraft carrier, IJN *Shinano*. All three were sunk near the end of the war without making any material contribution to Japanese defenses. There were to have been two more ships, but the resources available would not permit it. *Author's collection*

In 1912, the USS *Arkansas* and USS *New York* sported 14-inch, .45-caliber guns in their main batteries, but still retained the casemate guns and vertical-triple-expansion engines. However, as one class was being built, another was being designed that was even better.

The U.S. Navy contributed escort vessels to combat the U-boat menace and sent battleships to join in the North Sea Patrol. Of course, the battleships had to burn coal, as there was very little fuel oil available in Great Britain. As a result, the U.S. Navy's most modern battleships were kept near the American coastline, where there was plenty of fuel oil, and the older coal-burning battleships were sent to Europe. In a major world war, this simply would be unacceptable. Having modern warships and no fuel is a very basic error in logistics and could have meant the difference between defeat and victory. Fortunately, the sea war had all but ended by the time the United States entered the conflict. Of greater interest was the U.S. Navy's method of developing new battleships—in pairs, and the ships were designed sequentially. As soon as one class was developed, another was ready to be built with substantial improvements.

The classes of battleship in the first two decades of the twentieth century were:

1. USS *Florida,* 1911 (two ships)
2. USS *Wyoming,* 1912 (two ships)
3. USS *New York,* 1914 (two ships)
4. USS *Nevada,* 1916 (two ships)
5. USS *Pennsylvania,* 1916 (two ships), sister was the USS *Arizona*
6. USS *New Mexico,* 1918 (two ships)
7. USS *Maryland,* 1921 (three ships)
8. USS *South Dakota,* 1922 (six ships, all scrapped)

It was not until 1920, with the commissioning of the USS *Tennessee* and the USS *California,* that the ships adopted a rather revolutionary armored system. It was dubbed the "all-or-nothing plan." All battleships in the U.S. Navy utilized this concept up through the four-ship *Iowa* class. Forty-two battleships built since 1900 relied upon armor plate placed uniformly in as many areas as possible, with additional inches of steel on the turrets, conning tower, and engine uptakes. Other than the most obvious needs, armor plate found itself virtually everywhere. The all-or-nothing plan was based on heavily protecting those areas that were most important aboard the ship. The conning tower, turrets, ammunition magazines, and other vitals within the ship received the highest degree of armor. The balance of the ship received a great deal less armor, thus allowing for the most essential components of the ship to have the greatest protection.

The story of the *Bismarck* and its last cruise is well known. This 41,700-ton-full-load battleship mounted eight 15-inch guns in its main battery and twelve 5.9-inch weapons in the secondary. It had a maximum speed of 29 knots, and its primary role was that of locating and then decimating a fully loaded Allied convoy bringing vital food and munitions supplies to Europe. Without the constant flow of supplies from the United States, Great Britain had approximately six weeks before rations would be cut to the bone and infants and the elderly would begin to suffer from malnutrition. Britain had to deal with this threat to its lifeline from U-boats and surface warships. When the heavy cruiser *Prinz Eugen* and *Bismarck* made their breakout from Norway in late May 1941, it was with the intention of sinking Allied shipping and reducing supplies and equipment on the way to Russia and Great Britain. After the HMS *Hood* was sunk and HMS *Prince of Wales* was repulsed, the entire Royal Navy, including carriers, sought to kill this ship. Finally, on May 26, heavy units of the Home Fleet caught the *Bismarck* and repeatedly hit her with heavy shells and torpedoes. On May 27, in the early morning hours, the *Bismarck* was sunk. A major threat had been removed from the Atlantic lifeline. *Author's collection*

The American post-dreadnought, or fast battleship, USS *North Carolina* (BB-55) was one of two in a class, and mounted nine 16-inch guns. Shown here, she is preserved as a ship memorial and museum. Periodically, the *North Carolina* and other museum ships that are displayed in water must be dry-docked in order to sandblast the hull and give it a fresh coat of anti-fouling paint, in addition to other repairs and upkeep. *Author's collection*

There were nineteen battleships built from 1911 until 1923, and six more that had to be scrapped to comply with the 1922 Washington Naval Arms Limitation Treaty. Yet, after a building frenzy, from 1923 until 1941 the U.S. Navy did not introduce a single new battleship. However, in 1941, the USS *North Carolina* and USS *Washington* (designed in 1937 and with their keels laid) made their debut. They mounted nine 16-inch guns in three triple turrets and were capable of 28 knots. They were the direct precursors to the modern battleship. Closely following were the World War II–built ships of the *South Dakota* class (*South Dakota, Massachusetts, Indiana,* and *Alabama*), which also mounted nine 16-inch guns in three triple turrets and also had a top speed of 28 knots. The final class was the four-ship

Iowa class, with nine 16-inch guns and 33 knots. These were also the finest battleships ever built, which included the USS *Missouri* (BB-63). This same treaty applied to all nations in the naval arms race: Great Britain, France, Italy, the United States, and Japan.

During the interwar years, all nations that had been a signatory of the arms limitation treaties skirted around its rules to build bigger and more powerful ships. Even Germany violated the Versailles Treaty and built ships such as monsters like the *Tirpitz* and *Bismarck*. Not one nation raised any complaint! It was as if World War I was left unsettled by an armistice, and the next war, which was right around the corner, would finally settle accounts. The signatories were supposed to limit capital ships to 35,000 tons and a 16-inch main battery. This was patently ignored.

The USS *Alabama* (BB-60), silhouetted in the late afternoon sun in its berth in Mobile, Alabama, was another post-dreadnought, or fast battleship. It was one of four ships of the *South Dakota* class. Although it resembled the *Iowa* class, it only had a single funnel. Hurricane Katrina did much damage to the museum complex, and the cofferdam that held the *Alabama* was substantially eroded. After two years, it had been repaired. *Author's collection*

THE INTERWAR YEARS, BATTLESHIP CONSTRUCTION, AND TREATY VIOLATIONS

With the exception of Great Britain and United States, the naval powers viewed the Washington Naval Arms Limitation Treaty as something to be dishonored, and some countries practiced outright deception. The Italian navy exceeded the tonnage allowable and built ships of incredibly high speed. This proved to be their undoing, as their under-protected capital ships were collectively known as the "cardboard navy."

A provision of the treaties was that nations could improve their existing capital ships, and thus many found their way into dry docks for extended periods while they were modernized. Anti-torpedo bulges were fitted and additional antiaircraft weapons were added. All were converted to oil-burning ships, and coal-fired engines were a thing of the past. But, despite the improvements, they were still World War I ships,

and no match for determined pilots. This was proven over and over in the early days of World War II. Some nations made improvements in their older ships, but built newer and faster vessels for the future.

Like Italy, France did likewise and had an open competition with its neighbor over the speed of its capital ships. Of course, the worst offender was Japan, who had been insulted and lost face in the 1922 Washington Treaty. That agreement allowed Japan to construct a paltry amount of tonnage, thus putting a hamstring on any designs their militaristic government had in the Pacific and Pacific Rim. Accordingly, they built ships in secret that violated the 1922 treaty and others, and did not allow inspection of their activities. This was a double-edged sword, however, as they built three seagoing giants: the *Yamato*-class battleships. The Imperial Japanese Navy had intended to build five of these 72,802-ton 862.5-foot-long battleships. Only two, *Yamato* and *Musashi*, were commissioned,

The first plate of the USS *Missouri's* keel is riveted by Rear Adm. Clark H. Woodward. The new *Iowa*-class battleship is being built by the Brooklyn Navy Yard in New York. A riveting machine is being used, as opposed to a hot rivet and a jackhammer. Eventually, the *Missouri* was to have three bottoms. *Author's collection*

and the third, IJN *Shinano,* was converted to a huge aircraft carrier. It was promptly sunk by an American submarine while on sea trials. The remaining two were simply known as hull numbers 111 and 797, and never went any further.

The two battleships were designed in 1934, and ultimately commissioned in intensive secrecy in December 1941. They contributed little to the war effort in the first few years except their reputations, yet in April 1945, Operation Ten Go was devised to throw the Allies off Okinawa. The *Yamato* was fueled for a one-way trip and, according to the plan, would run herself on the Okinawa beach to become a stationary gun battery. With her nine 18.1-inch guns in the main battery and assorted smaller weapons, including 162 25mm antiaircraft guns, she would become a formidable fort. Before reaching her objective, the *Yamato* succumbed to American carrier planes and sank after repetitive strikes by torpedoes and bombs.

Likewise, the IJN *Musashi* was also dispatched. Faith in a weapon that was obsolete cost the Japanese over five thousand young sailors. Besides, the steel and resources used in the construction of these monoliths to a bygone age would have built at least ten small aircraft carriers and dozens of escort vessels. This is what happened when the battleship admirals had their way and did not look to the future.

Likewise, Germany lost both the *Tirpitz* and *Bismarck* early in the war. There was a place for the battleship, but it was no longer the most valuable weapon in the fleet. It had been supplanted by the aircraft carrier and later the submarine. Most leading naval authorities still did not want to admit this, and they looked forward to the day when the protection of a nation was wholly dependent on the outcome of huge sea battle wherein battleships would oppose each other and slug it out until the winner was left in command of the sea.

Margaret Truman, the daughter of Senator Harry Truman, christens the *Missouri* with champagne. The bottle is covered by a silver canister to prevent glass from hitting the bystanders. In just over eighteen months, the surrender ceremony ending World War II would be signed on her deck, and the *Missouri* would become the most famous battleship in the world. *Author's collection*

The ways have been coated with tons of oil, grease, and tallow to allow the ship to slide down as easily as possible. The *Missouri* is almost at the end of its run down the ways. Just prior to the launching, divers inspected the area behind the ways to ensure that there were no obstructions or items that might damage the hull as it moved into the water. *U.S. Navy*

The *Missouri* has moved into the river, and chains have been dropped to slow the progress of the ship out into the river. As can be seen, more chains will be dragged alongside the ship to slow it down so that it can be controlled by tugboats. *U.S. Navy*

Commissioning day for the USS *Missouri* (BB-63) was June 11, 1944. Hundreds of well-wishers and senior naval officers were on hand for one of the last commissionings of a battleship. Soon, the ship would go out on its sea trials, and then after any and all defects were remedied, it would be off to a war zone. *U.S. Navy*

INTERWAR BATTLESHIP PROGRAM

The final battleship built by the United States before the next war was the USS *West Virginia* (BB-48). It was commissioned on December 1, 1923, and it would be two decades before any other new capital ships joined the fleet. Despite the fact that the relatively new *West Virginia* joined the fleet, it was still a throwback to an era that was obsolete. And, incidentally, it was lost during the first minutes of the Japanese air attack on Pearl Harbor. Japanese aircraft utilizing torpedoes and armor-piercing bombs were more than a match for the elderly ships.

Of course, by the time of the Pearl Harbor attack, the world's navies had already witnessed a terrible defeat at Taranto Harbor when Royal Navy Swordfish torpedo bombers flying from an aircraft carrier attacked the shipping in the harbor. The tally was one battleship sunk and two severely damaged, as well as a light cruiser damaged. On an even greater scale was the attack on Pearl Harbor, with a large number of battleships sunk or damaged, as well as several cruisers and auxiliaries. And, three days later, the Royal Navy's Force Z was decimated while attempting to stave off the Japanese invasion of Malaya. A battleship, HMS *Prince of Wales*, and a battlecruiser, HMS *Repulse,* were caught at sea, and in less than an hour were sunk with very little loss to the enemy aircraft. The writing was on the wall: capital ships required substantial antiaircraft defenses to survive in modern combat at sea.

All of that was still in the future when the U.S. Navy began to sidestep the naval arms limitation treaties in the years preceding World War II. Japan walked out of the 1936 meeting of the League of Nations and proceeded to openly defy the international community with its new warships, whose displacements were far greater than the

The top of the armored conning tower aboard the USS *Missouri*. The thickness of the armor plate that makes up the tower was sufficient to protect the occupants from heavy shell hits. The armor is extremely high grade. Every battleship in the U.S. Navy has a similar arrangement, as do many foreign ships. The conning tower has slits cut in it to allow the occupants a limited view outside. *Author's collection*

treaty limitations, as were the guns, with shells up to 18.1 inches. Germany was not bound by the League of Nations, and without any real rules, proceeded to build warships such as the heavy, heavy *Deutschland*-class cruisers, which mounted six 11-inch guns and displaced well over sixteen thousand tons. This was a clear violation of the Versailles Treaty, as were the fifty-four-thousand-ton *Bismarck* and her sister ship, *Tirpitz*. Of course, Nazi submarines were now being built and launched with crews trained in the Soviet Union.

In other words, each nation that had subscribed to peace at the end of World War I was now rebuilding its military forces. It was too bad that many of the nations wasted time, effort, and resources on rebuilding warships from World War I to keep the battleship and battle cruiser in a prominent position in the fleet. This was done at the expense of ship types that would be needed in the upcoming war.

The United States did have a healthy program for building aircraft carriers, destroyers, submarines, and capital ships.

There were three battleship construction programs in the late 1930s. All were considered fast battleships, despite the speed range of 27 to 33 knots. The first was Battleship 1937, or the *North Carolina*, class, with the USS *North Carolina* (BB-55) as the class leader. The other ship in this class was the USS *Washington* (BB-56), and they closely resembled the *Iowa*s due to the two funnels.

At first, this class was to be sixty thousand tons and be able to transit the Panama Canal. The maximum gun size was to be 20 inches; however, there were substantial changes prior to settling on the design. The ship and class were authorized March 27, 1934; the keel was laid on October 27, 1937; and the first ship was launched on June 13, 1940.

It was a warm spring day on April 9, 1941, when the *North Carolina* was commissioned as the first battleship in the U.S. Navy since 1923.

North Carolina statistics
- Full-load displacement: 44,800 tons
- Construction costs: $76,885,750
- Overall Length: 728'9"
- Beam: 108'4"
- Armor: maximum thickness (turret face) 18"
- Crew complement: 2,500 wartime
- Main battery: nine 16-inch, .45-caliber Mk 6 guns (range: 40,600 yards, armor-piercing [AP] rounds)
- Secondary Battery: twenty 5-inch, .38-caliber dual-purpose (DP) guns, sixty 40mm guns; 36 20mm, .70-caliber single-barrel cannons
- Oil-fired geared turbines, 7,167 tons oil, 28 knots full speed
- Four screws, 121,100 horsepower

The USS *Washington* (BB-56) was very much like the *North Carolina* except for some minor capacities.

The primary defect in the *North Carolina* class was the speed at 28 knots. At one time, this battleship would have been considered a fast battleship, but with onset of the 33-knot aircraft carriers built in World War II, 30 or more knots were a necessity, and anything slower was unacceptable. The speed of the *North Carolina* class was designed based on concepts that were common during the period when the 1922 Washington Arms Limitation Treaty came into effect.

The exterior in front of the armored conning tower in the USS *Missouri,* which leads to the bridge. All of the communication systems were provided for, yet in the first days of the battleships, speaking tubes were used in place of radios, telephones, and such. *Author's collection*

Inside the armored conning tower, where the vision slits can easily be seen. In the center of the frame is a periscope that has its head on the rooftop of the tower and allows the command staff to get a full view around the ship during battle. *Author's collection*

The next battleship class was the four-ship *South Dakota* class, comprising the USS *South Dakota* (BB-57), USS *Indiana* (BB-58), USS *Massachusetts* (BB-59), and the USS *Alabama* (BB-60).

- Authorized: March 27, 1934
- Commissioned: March 20, 1942
- Crew complement: 2,500 wartime
- Full-load displacement: 35,000 tons
- Construction cost: $76,000,000
- Main battery: nine 16-inch, .45-caliber Mk 6 guns; range, 40,600 yards with AP rounds
- Secondary battery: sixteen 5-inch, .38 caliber guns in eight twin mounts; fifteen quad 40mm, .70-caliber machine guns; eight 20mm Mk 4 cannons
- Armor: 18" on turret fronts
- Length overall: 680', beam 108'2"

- Built by: New York Shipbuilding Camden, New Jersey
- Engines: geared turbines, 130,000 horsepower, 27 knots

These battleships, collectively known as the "Battleships 1939," were slower still than the *North Carolina*s. However, the *South Dakota* had a reputation for downing Japanese aircraft at a phenomenal rate, twenty-six in one raid alone. She was known as "Battleship X" or the "Big Bastard." Yet, she was heavily damaged during a gunfight with Japanese capital ships during the November 14–15, 1942, Naval Battle of Guadalcanal. After a shell disabled a series of circuit breakers, the *South Dakota* was reduced to manual control. During the time it took to repair the damage, the Japanese

Part of the turret of a 16-inch gun aboard the USS *Missouri*. Every precaution was taken to prevent a flare-up or explosion in one of the most dangerous locations in the world. *Author's collection*

battleship *Kirishima* and heavy cruisers *Takao* and *Atago* took her under fire at ranges less than six thousand yards. Luckily, the thirty-four Long Lance torpedoes launched at the *South Dakota* went off into the night. On the other hand, the Big Bastard was hit twenty-seven times during a twenty-three-minute period by heavy and moderate-sized shells. Most shells struck the poorly armored superstructure and did not impair the hull, engines, and overall fighting capability. The USS *Washington* came to the aid of the *South Dakota* and hit the *Kirishima* nine times with 16-inch armor-piercing shells. The *Kirishima*

was now a dying ship, and the *South Dakota* had been spared.

The Naval Battle of Guadalcanal has been touted as rivaling Jutland as a ship-to-ship duel. The morning after the battle was over, the area was littered with sinking and seriously damaged ships on both sides. It was one of the last episodes of battleship-versus-battleship combat. For all of the expense and effort put into battleship design, construction, and maintenance, it was a poor return on the investment. Many 1,500-ton submarines did more damage than most battleships during the entire war at sea.

THE IOWA CLASS AND THE FINAL BATTLESHIP EFFORT

The four-ship *Iowa* class was the final battleship offering by the U.S. Navy. There were to have been six ships, yet the USS *Illinois* (BB-65) and USS *Kentucky* (BB-66) were never completed. There was even talk and preliminary design of a larger class, the *Montana*, which was to have included the USS *Montana* (BB-67), USS *Ohio* (BB-68), USS *Maine* (BB-69), USS *New Hampshire* (BB-70), and the USS *Louisiana* (BB-71). The *Montana*s and any other larger battleships were never built and never will be built. The reign of the world's steel battleships came to end after a century of dominance.

The *Iowa* class is the finest battleship offering in the world, and the four ships, USS *Iowa* (BB-61), USS *New Jersey* (BB-62), USS *Missouri* (BB-63) and USS *Wisconsin* (BB-64), contributed much to the nation and the free world from World War II until the Persian Gulf War in 1991.

It seemed as if all of the lessons learned over the last hundred years were incorporated in the *Iowa* class, and what emerged was the quintessential battleship.

Iowa statistics
* Authorized: March 27, 1934–May 17, 1938
* Commissioned USS *Missouri* (BB-63), June 11, 1944
* Crew: 2,700, World War II service
* Displacement: 58,000 tons
* Construction cost: $100 million 1944, $496 million reactivation in the 1980s

"Broadway," or the longest passageway down through the horizontal of the ship, runs over three hundred feet, and there are a dozen-plus knee-knockers throughout its length. *Author's collection*

Shortly after the *Missouri* has moved into the Pacific, the ship fires its forward two turrets. To the right of the photograph, 2,700-pound armor-piercing projectiles can be seen on their way to their destination, up to twenty-four miles away. The accuracy using an analog computer was phenomenal, and still is in the twenty-first century. *U.S. Navy*

- Main battery: nine 16-inch, .50-caliber Mk 7 with a 41,600-yard range for 2,700-pound AP projectiles; service shells 1,900 pounds
- Main battery additions in 1980s: forty Mk 141 Harpoon surface-to-surface (antiship) missiles, eight Mk 143 Tomahawk (ABL) surface-to-surface (ground attack) missiles
- Secondary battery: twenty (later twelve) 5-inch, .38-caliber guns in twin mounts (range 17,306 yards, 54-pound projectile); fifteen quad-mount 40mm, .70-caliber guns (1.9815-pound shell); sixty 20mm single-mount machine guns (0.2716-pound shell, 450 rounds per minute); prior to 1980s, 20mm and 40mm removed
- Secondary battery, 1980s: four Mark 15 20mm Vulcan Phalanx CIWS (close-in weapons system)
- Armor: maximum thickness 18" on turret face plate
- Length: 887'3", beam: 108'3"
- Built by: New York Navy Yard, Brooklyn, New York
- Engines: Geared turbines, oil-fired boilers—212,000 shaft horsepower, 33 knots maximum speed
- Fuel capacity: 7,073 tons oil (2,121,900 gallons); burned 180 gallons per mile in transit, and often had to fuel up to four destroyers during rapid, high-tempo operations

The *Missouri* was launched on January 29, 1944, amid the cheers of thousands of people, and it was the first major event of this nature transmitted by television. The ship's sponsor, Margaret Truman, the daughter of Missouri's Senator Harry Truman, smashed the iconic champagne bottle on the huge ship's bow, and she began her slide into the river. It took the New York Navy Yard a little over four months to make the ship ready for commissioning, and on June 11, 1944, she became the USS *Missouri* (BB-63). It was a beautiful spring day for the ceremony, and it is certain that many wondered where this ship would go and what she would achieve. No one could predict that the *Missouri* would join the ranks of the greatest warships to fight for the United States. That was yet to come, and quite soon in the Pacific, because the Japanese had yet to be conquered.

The new battleship USS *Missouri* (BB-63) steams at speed for the war zone with its initial camouflage paint job. Based on word from the Pacific forward area, the ship required antiaircraft weaponry in every spare area of the deck, and redundancy was vital to shooting down determined swarm attacks of kamikazes. These were the first true guided missiles, and it would take more than human management of weapons to bring them down. Electronic assistance was a must, and this was also a foretelling of the future. *U.S. Navy*

CHAPTER THREE

SERVICE IN WORLD WAR II

THE "MIGHTY MO" OR "BIG MO" WAS THE third and final ship built that took the name USS *Missouri*. The *Iowa*-class battleship was ordered on June 12, 1940, and her keel laid on January 6, 1941, at the New York Navy Yard at Brooklyn, New York. She had been designed in 1938 by the Preliminary Design Branch of the Bureau of Construction and Repair (Navy Department) as a fast battleship, and at over 33 knots, the *Missouri* and her three sisters are the fastest battleships ever built. The *Missouri* was completed for launching on January 29, 1944, and commissioned as a U.S. Naval ship on June 11, 1944. The *Missouri* was the last of the *Iowa* class, and likely the last battleship to be built by any nation.

While beautiful, functional, and solid, the battleships have no value in modern warfare. The warship of today is designed to house electronics that have replaced the armor plate of the twentieth century, and missiles that far outrange any of the projectiles once fired by the *Iowa* class's 16-inch weapons. A Tomahawk missile has a range of over seven hundred miles, whereas a 16-inch rifle can throw a projectile just over twenty-five miles. There is no real comparison except the cost of the munitions. The 16-inch projectile is but a fraction of the cost of a Tomahawk cruise missile.

Fortunately, three of these giants have been preserved, and the fourth, the USS *Iowa*, is on

Lowering a shell from the main deck to the magazine below for one of the three triple-barrel 16-inch guns of an *Iowa*-class battleship—a time when caution was paramount. *U.S. Navy*

"donation hold" by the navy. This means that the fourth battleship will probably find a home in the near future. It would be a terrible shame for generations to come if all four of these ships were not preserved. As an aside, whenever I visit the *Iowa,* I make it a point of hitting the armored hull, with its 12.1-inch-thick steel. This steel is the most solid that I have ever touched. That alone is worth keeping these ships, as future generations need to see and feel the most tempered steel made by man.

The *Missouri* carried out its sea trials in Chesapeake Bay as well as an abbreviated shakedown cruise for the wartime crew of 2,700. Battle practice was also carried out in the Chesapeake Bay as part of the shakedown cruise, and on November 11, 1944, after repairs and modifications were completed at the Norfolk Navy Yard, the *Missouri* pointed her bow southward. Her first destination was San Francisco, where she would be fitted out as a fleet flagship. The *Missouri* was also exchanging the catapult-launched Vought OS2U Kingfisher scout aircraft for the Curtiss SC-1 Seahawk. The single-seat Seahawk was a much more powerful and high-performance aircraft.

Interestingly, her escorts to the West Coast were the two most elderly battleships in the U.S. Navy, the USS *Arkansas* (1912) and the USS *Texas* (1914). It was a very close fit as the new battleship went through the Panama Canal's locks: inadvertently, she kept a few pieces of concrete.

The work on the *Missouri* in San Francisco was completed on December 14, 1944, and then she and escort steamed for Ulithi, the U.S. Navy's massive

Ulithi Atoll and the world famous "Murderer's Row" of *Essex*-class aircraft carriers. From front to rear are the *Essex, Yorktown, Ticonderoga, Lexington,* and *Bunker Hill.* Many would suffer near-mortal damage from kamikaze attacks in the weeks to come. *Bruce Makoto Arnold*

Carrier pilots assemble to plan an attack to repel incoming Japanese aircraft from the Japanese home islands to Iwo Jima. The Hellcat and Corsair aircraft were the fleet's first line of defense, other than an early warning by picket destroyers stationed far out from the fleet—the loneliest and most dangerous duty in the navy. *U.S. Navy*

forward anchorage in the Pacific. There was a short stopover at Pearl Harbor from December 24, 1944, through January 2, 1945, and then she steamed for the West Caroline Islands and a rendezvous with Task Force 58. After a short stay with the fleet that had gathered in Ulithi Lagoon, the *Missouri* was assigned to escort the USS *Lexington* (CV-16) carrier group (Task Group 58.2) as part of Task Force 58.

Like the battleships that had preceded her in the Pacific, it was vital to have 20mm or 40mm antiaircraft weapons on every square foot of the deck possible. These weapons had proven themselves

quite capable against Japanese aircraft, and combined with the twenty 5-inch, .38-caliber guns in ten twin mounts, the entire package was formidable against attacking aircraft. The 5-inch guns could pour out up to twenty rounds per barrel, per minute and create a barrage over the ship. This was dependent on the capability of the gun crew and the shells being sent up from the magazine.

The overall system of antiaircraft fire-control electronics and manual processing worked exceptionally well. The search radars, such as the SK-2 air-search radar, would pick up and track

The six barrels of the number-one and -two 16-inch turrets are trained to port, and a firing exercise is about to be begin. The noise from these guns, especially in salvo, is unduplicated in any other venue, and particularly not in motion pictures. One has to be there to truly experience the raw power. *U.S. Navy*

targets at relatively great distances. The targets could be then identified as friend or foe, and when close enough to the *Missouri* for the Mk 37 secondary battery director to take over, the 5-inch mounts opened fire with proximity-fused projectiles. The proximity-fused shells had only to get within a certain distance of the target for it to explode, and was then generally lethal to the enemy aircraft. It was an entirely different ball game than the prewar open-mount 5-inch, .25-caliber guns backed up by .50-caliber machine guns.

In addition to 5-inch weapons, the *Iowa* class carried fifty-two single 20mm machine guns and twenty 40mm quad mounts with a total of eighty barrels. Of course, when World War II came to an end, the number of short-range antiaircraft guns was substantially reduced. However, the antiaircraft batteries aboard the *Missouri* and other modern cruisers and battleships were primarily designated to help protect the fast carriers.

On January 27, the *Lexington* task group put to sea with Adm. Marc Mitscher flying his flag

Two barrels have just erupted with 16-inch projectiles that are on their way toward a target. The other four barrels will soon be following with their own shooting. *U.S. Navy*

aboard the *Missouri*. Just over two weeks later, on February 16, the first air attacks were launched against the Japanese homeland since the Halsey-Doolittle Raid in April 1942.

STRIKING THE JAPANESE HOMELAND

Task Force 58 was aligned in five task groups, with Adm. Raymond Spruance as the overall commander in the heavy cruiser USS *Indianapolis* (CA-35). Task Group 58.2 was under the command of Rear Admiral Davidson and included the *Essex*-class carriers USS

Lexington (CV-16) and USS *Hancock* (CV-19), escorted by the battleships USS *Wisconsin* (BB-64) and USS *Missouri* (BB-63). This group also had two heavy cruisers and nineteen destroyers as a screen. Overall, Task Force 58 had a grand total of 118 warships at its disposal for the attack on the Japanese homeland.

There was great concern among the task force commanders and pilots that the Japanese would retaliate with kamikazes and fighter protection not seen in several months. As a consequence, the force had a substantially larger fighter defense to counter the threat. Each carrier contributed seventy-three Corsairs and Hellcats to this end, and reduced their air groups to thirty torpedo- or dive-bombing aircraft.

The underlying campaign was actually the attack and seizure of Iwo Jima. The carrier operations were scheduled between February 10 and March 10, 1945. It was important for Task Force 58 and its eleven large and five light carriers to be able to reduce the Japanese aircraft threat as much as was possible. Secondly, it would be another shock to Japanese morale to see carrier aircraft in large numbers striking areas near the country's principal city, Tokyo.

Of course, the long-range objective was to secure Iwo Jima and thus have a fighter and bomber base close to the Japanese home islands. Having Iwo Jima would save innumerable Army Air Forces lives and allow for fighter defenses both ways to the Japanese homeland. The P-51 Mustang fighter could carry enough aviation gasoline to make the trip and guard the B-29 bombers.

Five-inch, .38-caliber twin mounts open fire at night against radar-selected targets. The 5-inch guns had an effective range of thirteen miles and were dual purpose. Firing shells fitted with proximity fuses, they could provide a barrage that was lethal to incoming enemy aircraft and under optimum conditions could pour out twenty shells per barrel per minute. Of course, the gun crew had to be strong and very experienced. *U.S. Navy*

The targets at hand were various airfields and other military and industrial complexes near Tokyo Bay. On February 16, the task force, amidst great secrecy, had come within 125 miles southeast of Tokyo and 60 miles of the coast of Honshu.

Ironically, with the exception of one group, the Japanese were reluctant to do battle with the carrier fighters. In general, the American pilots hit their targets with relative ease. However, the weather did not cooperate for very long, and the attacks had to be curtailed. The weather was so cold that many of the aircraft guns actually froze up and refused to work. The carrier attacks scheduled to last into March were terminated, and the force headed for Iwo Jima.

On February 19, 1945, it was D-day for Iwo Jima. Battleships from World War I and those built just prior to World War II opened fire with their main and secondary batteries to help soften the island's defenses. This was no ordinary D-day for the marines that went ashore. They needed fire support continuously, and it was provided. The Japanese had years to prepare for the assault they knew was coming, so they were dug in deep. A series of tunnels, caves, and other natural defensive points assisted the Japanese defenders, and in some cases, only the heavy gunfire from the older battleships could destroy these emplacements. The fast battleships were more suited to escorting the carriers, whereas the older and slower battleships, such as *Texas* and *Nevada*, were superb for shore bombardment.

The Japanese aircraft that Task Force 58 was certain had been destroyed near Tokyo began to

Mount Suribachi on the barren island of Iwo Jima. In the foreground are two modern amphibious craft, but the island still looks like it did in 1945. No marine who attacked this island will ever forget Mount Suribachi, Joe Rosenthal's photograph of the flag being raised on its heights, and, almost as important, the black volcanic sand. *U.S. Navy*

appear on D-day, and up to fifteen aircraft began to harass the Task Groups. Fortunately, the nearby carriers could dispatch most if not all incoming enemy aircraft, but some "leakers" got through to the surface ships. This is when the *Missouri* shot down her first attacking aircraft, a twin-engine bomber code named Helen. The Mighty Mo hit the plane at 9,800 yards with 5-inch fire, and it was no more.

The *Missouri* did not come within sixty-five miles of Iwo Jima and was at the disposal of the carriers. The new battleship also doubled as fleet oiler, as the destroyers serving in the screen were fuel-thirsty ships. Consequently, the *Missouri* found itself fueling up to four destroyers at once, with two on each side. Further

air attacks on the Japanese homeland were drastically reduced due to severe weather conditions.

Weather had become a major factor in the plans of Task Force 58. Even ships the size and displacement of the *Missouri* felt the effects. In fact, the displacement caused the huge vessel to plunge deeply into the troughs of long swells and take green water from her bow to the base of the number-two 16-inch turret. At the end of a storm, it would not be unusual to see ammunition cases from 20mm and 40mm guns strewn about the deck and even on the roof of the number-one turret. One sailor in the deck gang, Seaman Dwyer, was washed over the side up forward. Fortunately, he was wearing a life preserver, and a

A grizzled and experienced gunner's mate works with a 40mm quad antiaircraft gun. This weapon was made under license from Sweden's Bofors Company, which still makes this type of weapon as well as others. It was one of the most effective antiaircraft guns produced during the war. Many nations used the single, dual, or quad models, depending on the needs of the ship or ground force. *U.S. Navy*

Gunners watch the sky from their 40mm quad mount aboard the *Missouri*. These guns were hand-fed with a four-shell clip, and after a number of firings, the barrels had to be replaced. *U.S. Navy*

destroyer rescued him about an hour later. He was returned to the ship the following day and was indeed a fortunate sailor. Of course, this weather also kept Japanese aircraft grounded; however, it held up a war that the Allies desperately wanted to see come to an end.

Finally, Iwo Jima was officially secured at 1800 hours on March 16, 1945. However, combat continued on the ground, and over the next ten days, the marines took 3,885 casualties. Even after March 26, when there were just a few defenders left, the diehard fanatics still kept the U.S. Army garrison troops on their toes. In the next few weeks, nearly two thousand more Japanese were killed, and

the army took a number of casualties during the post-mop-up fighting. The invasion of Iwo Jima resulted in 6,812 Americans killed in action. But, now the Allies could begin building an expanded air strip to accommodate B-29s that were damaged and needed to make emergency landings, and fighter aircraft to escort the bombers to and from their targets over Japanese home territory. This was the goal of capturing Iwo Jima, and the Allies had also pierced the inner defensive circle around the home islands. By the summer of 1945, over half of Iwo Jima was a series of airfields and revetments for aircraft. The next step was Okinawa, which the Allies hoped would be the climax of the war.

A "Zeke" turned kamikaze makes a run on the *Missouri,* and this photo was taken within a second of the plane striking the hull. Little real damage was done, and the remains of the pilot were given a full military burial. *U.S. Navy*

OKINAWA AND A GIANT STEP TOWARD VICTORY

Okinawa, or Okinawa Gunto, is one of a number of islands in the Ryukyus, and the closest to Japan, at a distance of 340 miles. The invasion of Okinawa and its capture was code named Operation Iceberg. The primary concerns were with the Japanese ground forces on Okinawa, estimated at one hundred thousand, their aircraft, and especially the Special Attack Corps (kamikazes).

D-day, or L-day in the actual plan, was set for April 1, 1945, and part of the softening of the island's defenses included hit-and-run shore bombardment by the *Missouri* and sisters *New Jersey* and *Wisconsin.* Five destroyers escorted the battleships, and Rear

Adm. L. E. Denfeld was in overall command of this bombardment. Another section of the coast was being hit by the battleships *Massachusetts* and *Indiana,* accompanied by six destroyers who pummeled targets with 16-inch and 5-inch gunfire.

The *Missouri*'s Seahawk was catapulted off the deck to act as a gunfire spotter. The attack began on March 24, and the ship fired at shore targets at ranges from 17,500 to 20,000 yards. The method employed in firing the projectiles resulted in a devastating plunging fire on a variety of targets. The *Missouri* fired 180 16-inch shells, and the crew was ecstatic because they were not acting as an overbuilt antiaircraft platform. The *Missouri* was behaving like a battleship! The battleship's gunfire ignited a large ammunition dump and destroyed several heavy-gun and antiaircraft gun emplacements, barracks, and an observation post. All in all, the selective bombardment was quite effective.

As to the landing site on Okinawa, it was the turn of the older battleships to tear up the beach. The fast battleships were with the carriers again. This time, the kamikazes went after the *Missouri*—well, at least one did. On April 11, a single-engine "Zeke" suicide plane headed for the *Missouri's* bridge. Crewmen attempted to crowd behind the armored citadel or conning tower, but it all happened so quickly that few had time to think. The plane struck the ship along the starboard armored side three feet below the main deck, yet did no material damage to the ship. The actual striking point was near the aft starboard quarter. It hit the *Missouri* with such force that the plane exploded and shattered. Its bomb failed to explode, which likely would have done more than superficial damage. Most of the pilot and aircraft went into the sea, except for the aluminum wing, some wreckage, and a portion of the mutilated pilot, which were strewn on the aft part of the ship. The wing was later cut up for souvenirs aboard ship. The other most interesting part of the Zeke was one of its machine guns, which was thrown

A machine gun from the kamikaze has been impaled on the barrels of a 40mm quad gun near where the aircraft struck. It made a great souvenir. *U.S. Navy*

toward a 40mm mount and impaled on a barrel. The remains of the pilot were given a military burial at sea as a sign of respect.

From a distance, many of the other ships thought the *Missouri* had been more severely damaged, yet it was just a temporary gasoline fire from the aircraft. It was soon out, and the minor damage repaired. It proved that a well-armored, fast warship that had sufficient modern antiaircraft defenses could ward off enemy aircraft. Of course, this was not the only attack by kamikazes on the battleship. Throughout April it seemed that the ship was at general quarters most of each day, and on April 16 another Zeke made a run on the stern and exploded in the ship's wake. However, the fantail was hit with a lot of shrapnel and debris. Two seamen were wounded during this attack.

Admiral William F. "Bull" Halsey Jr. took command of the Third Fleet, and his flagship was to be the USS *Missouri*. He and his staff boarded the ship on May 18, 1945. Most of the Allied military leaders fully expected that an invasion of the Japanese home islands would be necessary. If that were to be the case, the casualties would be incalculable. One estimate was a million Allied troops would be killed or wounded in the operation to subdue the Japanese.

Of course, Okinawa was still not completely secured, and the *Missouri* opened fire with her 16- and 5-inch weapons on caves that were suspected hideouts for Japanese troops and guns. The area was near the city of Naha, and Admiral Halsey wanted the Japanese to know he was back: the 16-inch shells were his calling cards!

Men aboard the *Missouri* examine the wing from the suicide plane. Most of the aircraft went over the side, but the wing was clipped off and landed on the deck. Later, the wing piece was cut up for crew souvenirs. *U.S. Navy*

OKINAWA SECURED AND THE MISSOURI'S FINAL STRIKE ON JAPAN

The battle to secure Okinawa actually went on until the 7th of September, yet weeks before that, the vast majority of the island was in Allied hands. There were pockets of resistance. However, the real battle was yet to come: the seizure of the home islands and perhaps the capture of the Son of Heaven—the Emperor.

The U.S. Navy's casualties in this battle totaled 32 ships sunk, 368 ships damaged, 763 aircraft lost, and 4,900 personnel killed. The Tenth Army lost 7,613 killed, 31,807 wounded, and 26,000 non-battle casualties. Overall, it was the most costly campaign in the history of World War II in the Pacific. However, it signaled the end for the Japanese Empire, and the realists were aware that it was just a matter of time.

Everywhere it seemed that the war was almost over. Only the fanatics would prolong the agony. The actual detailed plans for the defense of the home islands had been discovered aboard the cruiser IJN *Nachi,* which had been sunk in November 1944 in Manila Bay. Divers from U.S. Navy salvage tugs examined tons of material brought up from the officers' quarters aboard this ship, and part of the haul included detailed instructions on the defenses. They were formidable and included using children with spears and spikes to impale American soldiers. It also included instructions on summarily executing all prisoners of war in Japan. It was in part from examining these plans that the Allies arrived at the estimate that they would suffer a million casualties in an invasion of the home islands.

Smoke drifts behind the *Missouri.* A quick fire started from the kamikaze's gasoline tank, but it was soon put out. The smoke made the hit look far worse than it actually was. *U.S. Navy*

The *Missouri* opens fire on the steel works on the Nihon Steel Company and Wanishi Ironworks in Murotan, Hokkaido. In one instance, the ship fired three nine-gun salvoes at the huge cranes in the steelyard, and they became tangled messes of iron. After a while, optical sighting was impossible due to the smoke and dust. *U.S. Navy*

The *Missouri* and seven other fast battleships had one last thrust to make on Japan before awaiting the outcome of other international events that might accelerate the surrender. On July 1, 1945, the attack on the Japanese home islands by eight of the ten fast battleships was the result of Admiral Halsey demanding "battleship work for battleships." Admiral Halsey led the ships on an anti-shipping strike; however, they chose to attack the Nihon Steel Company and the Wanishi Ironworks at Murotan, Hokkaido. The *Missouri* let loose 297 high-explosive (HE) shells at the target, including three full salvoes by the nine 16-inch guns at the overhead cranes at the plants. Seen through the high-grade optics, the plant was devastated, and the battleships certainly had their final hurrah as battleships in a war dominated by the

RIGHT The *Missouri* cruises at high speed, from an angle off the port bow. Forward in the very front of the bow were two single-mount 20mm antiaircraft guns. This was also a rather dangerous location, because a wave or series of swells could wash a man overboard. Most wise sailors wore a harness and a life preserver. One who did not wear a lifeline was washed down the deck and over the side. An hour later, he was picked up by a trailing destroyer; he was very, very fortunate. *U.S. Navy*

An excellent image of the battleship as she steams in the Pacific. All of the secondary guns appear to be at the ready as well as the antiaircraft guns. It was not unusual for ships to be at general quarters for several hours each day. This was particularly true where kamikazes were known to be active. *U.S. Navy*

aircraft carrier since December 7, 1941. The attacks on the Japanese homeland continued during the nights of July 17 and 18 on industrial and military-supported targets in Honshu. The home waters now belonged to the *Missouri* and the other fast battleships.

The Army Air Force then dropped the second nuclear weapon, this time on Nagasaki, Japan. This attack had a profound effect on the Japanese imperial leadership that the militaristic fanatics could not overcome. There was now the probability of surrender, providing the emperor was not harmed.

Despite this, kamikazes still attacked the fleet, and the *Missouri* fired almost every gun that would bear on the targets. No damage was sustained, and on August 15, Admiral Halsey received the word at 0745: the war was over, and the Allies had been victorious. The USS *Missouri* was to be chosen for the honor of hosting the surrender ceremonies in Tokyo Bay. President Franklin Roosevelt had died earlier and never lived to see the ultimate glory of which he was a supreme architect. However, he was not far from the minds and hearts of those who actually knew.

A large mural is painted on the forward bulkhead in the wardroom of the *Missouri* to show its operations since commissioning. Ultimately, it will be for the public to see what the battleship has accomplished in World War II. *U.S. Navy*

The *Missouri* (right) is transferring two hundred officers and men to her sister ship USS *Iowa,* who will later make up a major landing party with companies from other battleships. The party will seize and begin examining the huge Yokosuka Naval Base. *U.S. Navy*

CHAPTER FOUR

JAPANESE SURRENDER AND POSTWAR YEARS

WITH THE HORN BLOWING AND THE *Missouri's* whistle also on full, Admiral Halsey had his four-star flag out on the mast. Unfortunately, the whistle was somewhat corroded, and its deafening noise would not stop for two minutes. The significance of the flag was that it was rarely flown, so as not to alert wary kamikazes that the *Missouri* had high-ranking staff aboard.

At 11:11 a.m., the noise died down as the actual belief that it was true began to sink in: forty-four months and seven days of war were finally over. This meant not being frightened every day, even if it was a latent fear.

The war in the Pacific should never have taken place. It was the brainchild of Imperial Japanese Army hotheads against conservative civilian leaders and many high-ranking naval officers. It was also in retaliation for perceived racial discrimination by America and the Washington Naval Arms Limitation Treaty. That treaty did treat the Japanese military in a very cavalier fashion.

Yet, once the Japanese decided upon war with the West, it was too late to fight the inevitable. There was the issue of cowardice and violating the national spirit, so all who once opposed that concept of attacking the U.S. fleet at Pearl Harbor quickly changed their minds and jumped on the bandwagon. For the Japanese military and civilian population, it

Japanese naval personnel and Tokyo and Sagami Wan harbor pilots provide information on where any minefields are located and other obstructions that might pose a problem for the large number of capital ships entering the area. Searching the Japanese netted several small knives and other quasi-weapons. *U.S. Navy*

The USS *Missouri,* followed by the USS *Iowa* and flanked by the USS *Nicholas* (DD-449), enters Tokyo Bay fully armed and ready for anything. The stress aboard these ships could have been cut with a knife. Nothing happened of concern. *U.S. Navy*

was a horrible and devastating decision that left the nation nearly in complete ruin. However, the twin nuclear explosions at Hiroshima and Nagasaki, plus the B-29s that roamed the skies at will, convinced cooler heads that the war was lost. It was not just the horror of the atomic weapons that tipped the balance toward surrender. The aircraft carriers of the U.S. Navy roamed at will around the home islands, and their air groups could bomb and strafe any target without real fear of reprisal. The Japanese military and civilian population were in essence held prisoner day and night by heavily armed aircraft. The Japanese were still building 1,700 aircraft per month, but this was of no value when every movement had to be preceded by a quick look to the sky. No amount of fanaticism or supreme belief in the power of the emperor would reverse complete and utter defeat that was just weeks away.

The battleship USS *Missouri* had been chosen virtually by groundswell in the United States as the ship destined to host the surrender activities. Washington insiders, reporters, columnists, and such printed or stated that the *Missouri* was to be the ship where it would all end. Men aboard the ship received letters from loved ones plus press clippings that seemed to confirm that the *Missouri* would be the location of the surrender and, as such, the site of one of the greatest diplomatic events in the history of mankind.

To this end, two hundred officers and men had been transferred to the battleship *Iowa* from the *Missouri* to act as a landing party, as part of a naval expeditionary force to occupy the giant naval base at Yokosuka, the air station at Atsugi, and other important installations in the Tokyo region. Battleships *Indiana, Massachusetts, Wisconsin,* and *Alabama* made similar manpower contributions for the first landing party in Japan. This also freed up space aboard the *Missouri* for the large number of visitors expected.

When men at war were used to seeing sights rarely seen elsewhere, it was quite a surprise to see a beautiful, hand-tooled saddle sent over by highline from the high-speed transport USS *Gosselin* (APD-126). The Chamber of Commerce of Reno, Nevada, had sent it as a gift to Admiral Halsey to ride the emperor's legendary white horse. Bales of hay were sent over as well.

On August 14, President Truman received a formal confirmation from the Japanese emperor that all of the demands in the surrender package were agreeable, with minor changes. The time in Washington, D.C., was 1550. Gen. Douglas MacArthur was to be supreme commander of all Allied powers. Japanese representatives were to meet him in Manila to establish the process for the surrender. Two aircraft painted white with green crosses flew the Japanese delegation to Ie Shima to transfer to an Army Air Force transport plane. In Manila, the dates and times were settled upon for the formal capitulation and the surrender of the Japanese military. Still, there were those Japanese who could not stomach the thought of surrender and on VJ Day alone, combat air patrols from the carriers and destroyer antiaircraft gunfire knocked down thirty-eight attacking Japanese aircraft,

The USS *Missouri* would host the surrender ceremony in Tokyo Bay adjacent to Sagami Wan with other capital ships; however, the aircraft carriers would remain at sea to provide air cover in the instance of any difficulties. They were also going to provide a demonstration of Allied air power over the *Missouri*, which included B-29s from the U.S. Army Air Forces.

Of course, safely entering Tokyo Bay necessitated information from local Japanese naval officers and harbor navigation pilots. The Japanese destroyer IJN *Hatsuzakura* brought the officials out to the destroyer USS *Nicholas* (DD-449) and then by highline to the *Missouri*. After the transfer was made, the little Japanese ship made a minor error in where it was to take station. The *Missouri's* commanding officer convinced the Japanese captain to encourage compliance by training ten 5-inch guns and 40mm mounts on his ship.

The eleven delegates selected by the Japanese government and the emperor from the navy, army, and civilian branches of the government are here to represent the nation at the surrender table. The individual that signed the 18 x 12-inch document first was Foreign Minister Mamoru Shigemitsu, who walked with a pronounced limp. He was wearing a wooden left leg, having lost his leg in 1933. *U.S. Navy*

A General Douglas MacArthur, supreme Allied commander, sits at the surrender table and signs the document with five pens. He is attended by Lt. Gen. Jonathan Wainwright, U.S. Army, and British Lt. Gen. Sir Archibald Percival. *U.S. Navy*

The ceremony is now over, and the Japanese delegation is leaving the *Missouri* to board their transportation ashore. It had been a somber event, yet when the Japanese left, all thoughts of sailors, airmen, marines, and soldiers turned to going home. The war was over. *U.S. Navy*

THE SURRENDER PROCEDURE AND CEREMONY

It was only natural that many felt that the surrender was an elaborate ruse to destroy the Allied fleet. Certain Imperial Army staff generals and Admiral Toyoda of the Naval Ministry were not convinced that the damage done by the atomic blasts was that critical, and that the Allies had no other similar weapons. Even one of the imperial family, Prince Takamatsu, had to visit Atsugi Airfield to keep the remaining kamikazes from attacking the *Missouri* when she entered Tokyo Bay. The pilots had been boasting of this plan and could not subject their nationalistic fervor to the emperor's directives until confronted by the imperial family. Fortunately, nothing happened, and the surrender ceremony proceeded as planned.

Treachery had happened before, so every precaution possible was being taken.

To prepare for the ceremony, scores of sailors from the *Missouri*'s crew were pressed into acting roles to practice the entrance and exit of all of the high-ranking officers and the Japanese representatives. After all, this was something that none of the participants had ever done in the past, and there was a certain theatrical flair to it. It had to be the height of officialdom, and the seriousness of the occasion could not in any way be marred. So, practice went on until it was nearly perfect. Actually, during the proceedings, there was only one noticeable mistake in protocol: A Russian photographer attempted to sneak into a forbidden area to capture the moment on film. A rather burly chief boatswain's mate prevented this from happening.

Personnel aboard nearby ships were aghast when they saw a nineteen-year-old seaman climb up the accommodation ladder to the *Missouri*'s deck, and a flag officer's gun salute was fired, and a four-star army general's flag was hoisted. This went on for hours until the entire process was fine-tuned.

The surrender document was drawn up on parchment paper well over a century old, located in a monastery in Manila. The ceremony was quite brief as the signers from the Allied powers stepped forward and the Japanese signers did likewise to end the war formally. The sole speech was by General MacArthur, and brief at that. The instrument was an unconditional surrender with some modifications to enable future governance by the supreme commander, who would be MacArthur. It had been worked out and agreed upon before this formal gathering took place. The emperor would not be present, as he was a godlike figure to his people.

Promptly at 0900 hours on September 2, the Allied and Japanese dignitaries and others gathered aboard the *Missouri* to carry out this final task. A U.S. destroyer brought them to the battleship. A small table from the crew's mess was set up on a veranda for the actual signing, and level of importance dictated where a guest would be allowed to participate or view the proceedings. After General MacArthur signed for the Allies (using five pens), he gave souvenir pens to Lt. Gen. Jonathan Wainwright and Lt. Gen. Arthur E. Percival; the rest were for family and U.S. archives. The two generals had been the commanders of the Philippines and Singapore, respectively, who were forced to surrender in 1942 and spent the war in captivity.

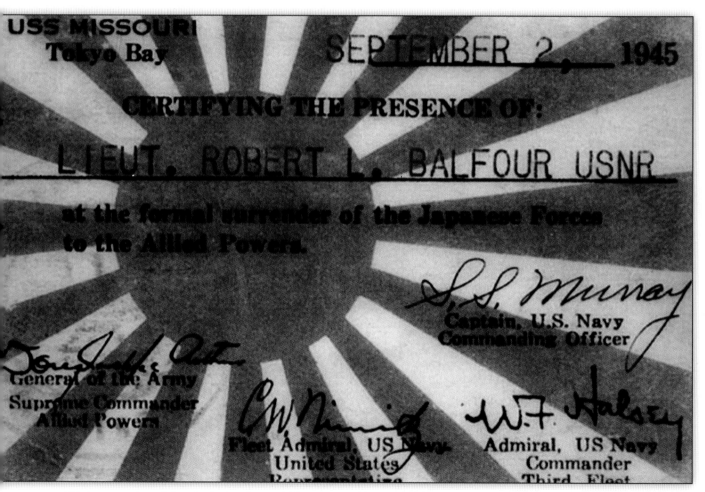

This is a souvenir card given to all who witnessed this ceremony. This was owned by Lt. Robert Balfour, USNR. *U.S. Navy*

A massive aerial demonstration was conducted over the *Missouri* to ensure that the Japanese never forgot the power brought to their shores to guarantee victory. The noise was so loud that no one could hear until the aircraft had passed. *U.S. Navy*

First, the Japanese signers affixed their names to the documents, one in English, the other in Japanese. Next came the Allied powers:

- General MacArthur, supreme Allied commander (first before the Japanese or Allied powers)
- United States of America: Fleet Adm. Chester W. Nimitz
- China: Gen. Hsu Yung-chang
- United Kingdom: Adm. Sir Bruce Fraser
- Soviet Union: Lt. Gen. Kuzma Derevyanko
- Australia: Gen. Sir Thomas Blamey
- Canada: Col. Lawrence Moore-Cosgrove
- France: Gen. Jacques Le Clerc
- Netherlands: Adm. C. E. L. Helfrich
- New Zealand: Air Marshal L. M. Isitt

In just twenty-five minutes, it was over, and the Japanese delegation left the *Missouri* for the mainland of Japan.

Five days after the surrender had been signed, General MacArthur went ashore to the American embassy and hoisted the American flag. It was the same flag flown over the U.S. Capital on December 7, 1941.

LEFT The Japanese delegation is now aboard the destroyer USS *Landsdowne* (DD-486) on their way from the ceremony. The foreign minister leads the group to the area where they will wait to go ashore. *U.S. Navy*

BELOW March 2006, and the USS *Missouri* is now a museum ship in Pearl Harbor. This roped-in area is where the surrender was signed. It is a great irony that the ship now sits on Battleship Row, just a few hundred yards from the USS *Arizona* (BB-39): where the war began and where it ended. *Author's collection*

A hand-tooled saddle made in Reno, Nevada, for Admiral Halsey to ride the Japanese emperor's white horse when the Allies seized Japan. Halsey never had use for this saddle, as he came back to the United States shortly after the surrender ceremony. *U.S. Navy*

Victory in war and in the Pacific had been achieved by the grace of God and the sacrifice of thousands of Allied military personnel. For a brief period, there was a euphoria that reassured the world that there would be no more wars.

On September 5, the USS *Missouri* left for Guam on her way back to the United States. Her role in history had been assured for all time.

The plaque that now is attached to the spot where the surrender occurred states:

> U.S.S. *Missouri*
> Latitude 35 degrees 21 minutes 17 seconds North
> Longitude 139 degrees 45 minutes 16 seconds East
>
> OVER THIS SPOT ON 2 SEPTEMBER 1945
> THE INSTRUMENT OF FORMAL SURRENDER
> OF JAPAN WAS SIGNED THUS BRINGING
> TO A CLOSE THE SECOND WORLD WAR
>
> THE SHIP AT THAT TIME WAS AT ANCHOR
> IN TOKYO BAY

By 1950, within five years of the end of World War II, there were cries in Congress for the wholesale scrapping of America's battleships. The war had driven home the lesson that the aircraft carrier, airplane, submarine, and many other vessel classes were war winners. The battleship was an expensive, labor-intensive war machine that no nation could afford. Even Great Britain, who once commanded the seas with battleships and battle cruisers, did so no longer. The United States had a number of battleships preserved in mothballs, and at least one on active duty. Many of the mothballed ships are still in existence as museum ships located in harbors all around the coastal United States.

One of these is the USS *Missouri* (BB-63), and as fate would have it, she became the most famous battleship in the fleet and literally in the nation's history. However, an embarrassing, and potentially battleship-killing incident on January 17, 1950 caused a great deal of humiliation and unnecessary hardship to the navy when the world's most powerful battleship slowly slid up on the sands that make up Thimble Shoals in Chesapeake Bay. Then, the sixty-thousand-ton ship was hard aground and held firm by the suction of the

Quartermaster Second Class Bevin E. Travis was at the wheel when the *Missouri* slid onto the mud bank on January 17, 1950. The grounding was not his fault or that of anyone except the captain and watch officers. *Treasure Island Museum/San Francisco Center for the Book*

sand and water. Prying this beautiful icon loose would consume the best minds and resources. At the same time, the opponents of the battleship were ecstatic

HARD AGROUND: ANATOMY OF A SHIPWRECK

In the five years that followed the end of World War II, the *Missouri* carried out a number of assignments, including midshipmen-training cruises and flag-showing abroad. There was a new conflict brewing simply termed the "Cold War," and the battleship played a very small role in this new phenomenon in international politics. It was a war of words and territorial expansion through the spread of ideology backed up by modern military hardware. Intercontinental ballistic missiles, electronic countermeasures, atomic bomb–carrying heavy bombers, and the submarine supplanted the battleship

The USS *Missouri* rests on Thimble Shoals in Chesapeake Bay. The sixty-thousand-ton battleship had slid up on a mud and sand shoal in broad daylight at fifteen knots. It was not until the ship had advanced over half its length on the mud bank that the captain and others realized that they were in trouble. *Treasure Island Museum/San Francisco Center for the Book*

even more than the aircraft carrier had during World War II. Keeping battleships in commission was an expensive proposition, and any time that the navy made an embarrassing mistake, it detractors were quick to point out the foolishness of the American taxpayer having to foot the bill for obsolete military hardware. Besides, the American public was crying out for the luxuries that made life in the United States the envy of the world. Thousands of washing machines, automobiles, kitchen appliances, and other consumer products could be made from the scrap metal of a

single battleship. The military strongly objected to this argument and did everything to maintain its strength. This was especially important in view of the new threat of worldwide Communism. However, there were those who did not see this as being that serious a peril and wanted household goods.

Although many captains were aspiring to command big-deck carriers, it was well known that being assigned the command of a battleship was still a step up for a captain who aspired to flag rank. On December 10, 1949, Capt. William

The *Missouri* rides high on Thimble Shoals with no immediate hope of freedom. *Treasure Island Museum/San Francisco Center for the Book*

U.S. Navy barges and tugs from the Norfolk Navy Yard begin the tedious job of offloading ammunition, powder bags, and anything that was portable from the *Missouri*. The goal was to lighten the ship as much as possible, to ease the way when it was finally determined that the tide was right to pull the ship off the shoal. *Treasure Island Museum/San Francisco Center for the Book*

The first real attempt to dislodge the stranded ship with a series of tugs on January 31, 1950, is a failure. Far more equipment and supplies have to be removed, and more horsepower in the form of tugs is required for a successful effort. *Treasure Island Museum/San Francisco Center for the Book*

D. Brown assumed command of the *Missouri,* one of the last remaining battleships still on active service. Within a few days the battleship left the Portsmouth Navy Yard for its trials off the coast. She returned on December 23, in time for Christmas ashore. The officers and crew began to acclimate themselves to their new commanding officer, who, like any, had idiosyncrasies and different methods compared to the previous captain. Captain Brown was a competent ship handler; however, his experience was limited to small, destroyer-type vessels. He also demonstrated a tendency toward micromanagement, with a consequent inability to delegate tasks and responsibilities to subordinates. This tendency would contribute to the tragedy that was about to befall the *Missouri* at the height of its popularity.

In early January 1950, the *Missouri* was alerted for duty near Guantanamo Bay, Cuba, where she and a number of other ships would be engaged in annual maneuvers and exercises. Her date of departure from the Norfolk Navy Yard was set for January 17, 1950, after being fully provisioned and loaded with ammunition. Just prior to her departure, Brown was notified that his new command was to carry out a voluntary, collateral mission. It was optional in that Brown could refuse based on operational or other compelling reasons. Since he acknowledged the request, he was to take the *Missouri* through an expressly marked channel near the harbor exit that was strewn with specially placed acoustic cables. The navy was attempting to develop a system of identifying shipping by their propeller signatures. Ultimately, this would be a highly valuable method of identifying various warships. The battleship propeller and other engine noises would be recorded as she steamed over the cables near Old Point Comfort. The run was charted and the channel prominently and thoroughly marked with buoys.

Unfortunately, two of the five marker buoys indicated on the chart had been removed, and the navigating staff aboard the *Missouri* was unaware of this change. This was to be a tragic and horribly embarrassing error, and it was but a foreshadowing of a series of errors that always seem to be present in all shipping disasters.

The *Missouri* left her mooring at 0725 and stood out of the harbor under the command of a local pilot. Conning a 60,000-ton battleship was far more difficult than a 2,200-ton destroyer, as Captain Brown would soon discover.

The weather presented no problem, and at 0749 the harbor pilot bid the giant ship farewell and handed it over to the ship's captain. The *Missouri* carried on toward the test range at a slow and manageable speed. The executive officer, Cmdr. George Peckham, remarked that the ship appeared to be heading toward two red markers that signified shoal waters on the chart. The *Missouri* drew thirty-seven feet fully loaded, which was far too much for the depth of water near the red warning markers.

At 0812, Captain Brown compounded what was to become a serious error in communication. He ordered the ship's speed increased to fifteen knots so as to give the rudders greater purchase and far greater maneuverability. Shortly after increasing the engine speed, he was alerted that an orange and white marker buoy was ahead. He was then counseled that the ship could pass to the starboard of the buoy, when in fact the ship should have kept the buoy to its port side. Two spar buoys now appeared off the bow, which was assumed to signify the end of the course, but actually signified shoal water at a depth of fourteen feet. Radar readings also showed danger, but they were ignored.

By now, even the helmsman knew that the great ship was in trouble. Quartermaster Second Class Bevin E. Travis could feel the wheel becoming sluggish, and the ship was involuntarily slowing down. The huge ship was slowly and almost imperceptibly riding up into a mud and sand bank. It was 0817, and the *Missouri* had now slid up on a mud bar or shoal for three-quarters of her length. Her black boot top, the stripe painted at the waterline, was now several feet out of the water at the bow, and the engines had been shut down due to sand clogging her intakes. She was now hard aground off Thimble Shoals and in plain view of the shore, the navy, media, and her most ardent detractors. It was no longer a question if a disaster had happened: it was whether the ship would become a permanent fixture (*Missouri* Shoals?) or if she could be quickly refloated in reasonably good condition.

By 0830 a request was made that all available tugs be summoned to pull the stranded ship off the mud, which was deferred until the situation could be

The *Missouri* was not the only fast battleship to run aground. In August 1951, the USS *Wisconsin* grounded near Edgewater, New Jersey. Divers were put over the side to assess the damage. The hull and propellers were sound, and the battleship was pulled loose within two hours. Aircraft carriers also have had the same difficulties, as did the USS *Enterprise* (CVN-65) in San Francisco Bay. Although she only touched bottom for a short time, her captain's career was over. *Treasure Island Museum/San Francisco Center for the Book*

Finally, on February 1, 1950, the great ship is pulled loose, using almost all of the salvage resources on the East Coast. *Treasure Island Museum/San Francisco Center for the Book*

The *Missouri's* band plays the "Missouri Waltz" to tell its crew that the ship is again afloat. *Treasure Island Museum/San Francisco Center for the Book*

assessed. Fortunately, salvage resources and the services of one of the great salvage masters were available. Rear Admiral Homer Wallin assumed command of the salvage effort and initiated a five-part plan:

- Remove all possible weight
- Provide buoyancy with pontoons
- Remove mud and sand from around ship with water jets
- Use brute pulling and pushing force
- Dredge a channel for the escape.

There were five major attempts to free the battleship, and the first four were failures. It was going to take far more than simply pulling the lightened ship off the shoals. The *Missouri* was actually trapped by a suction caused by being slid into mud. It was necessary to overcome this suction with a great deal of power.

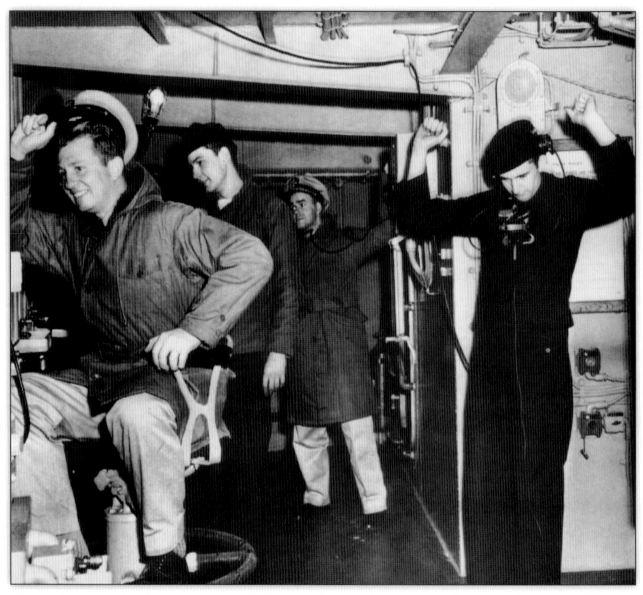

Officers and men celebrate as the ship gathers speed leaving the mud bank shortly after 0700 on February 1. Hundreds of naval officers breathed a sigh of relief, but the damage to the battleship as a fleet unit had been done, and it would take decades for the battlewagons to regain their esteem. *Treasure Island Museum/San Francisco Center for the Book*

Everything possible was done as quickly as possible to remove the spectacle of the *Missouri* hard aground. Work proceeded on a twenty-four-hour basis. Finally, the big effort consisted of five tugs pulled alongside, six pulling astern, and three swinging the bow to facilitate movement. Two salvage ships were connected astern, and seven yard tugs held the other vessels in place. Kedge anchors were out and used as part of the big pull. Finally, on February

1, 1950, just seventeen days after the *Missouri* slid aground, the pulling and pushing power freed the ship on the fifth attempt, and with the assistance of twenty-three vessels, she moved into the regular ship channel. There was some difficulty with the hull being held by an old buried anchor, but this was overcome, and the *Missouri* was towed to the dry dock formerly occupied by her uncompleted sister, the USS *Kentucky.* Contrary to her detractors who had hoped for serious damage, the *Missouri* was soon fit for sea.

A formal court of inquiry was held in the wake of this disaster, and the blame ultimately fell on the shoulders of Captain Brown and three subordinates. Brown was found guilty of negligence and suffered the loss of 250 numbers on the promotion list. This meant that he would not be promoted while on active duty. Other officers received lesser penalties, and the incident was formally closed.

LESSONS LEARNED

All officers who aspired to command any size of ship learned a vital lesson from the grounding of the USS *Missouri*. It is imperative to know the lay of the land, and trust nothing to providence. The *Missouri* should never have touched bottom had her captain and watch officers been savvy about the charted channel, and when the markers were discovered to be missing, the ship should not have entered the area. Actually, no ship should ever run aground, and the punishment for such a mistake is severe. In this instance, a battleship and its crew were far more valuable than a propeller-signature test.

The 1950 grounding was a disaster, but just one in passing. It also proved that the navy is highly adept at salvage. The USS *Missouri* will not be known for her grounding, but will be remembered for her value to the U.S. Navy and the nation on the international stage.

The USS *Missouri* has completed its voyage from Japan via Guam, Pearl Harbor, and Norfolk and has arrived in New York Harbor for a massive Navy Day celebration. President Truman and family have been brought aboard by the destroyer USS *Renshaw* (DD-499), moored to the starboard side of the battleship. *U.S. Navy*

CHAPTER FIVE

THE COLD WAR BEGINS

ON SEPTEMBER 5, 1945, JUST THREE DAYS AFTER the momentous occasion of receiving the surrender of the Japanese Empire, the USS *Missouri* moored next to the battleship *South Dakota,* and Admiral Halsey's flag was transferred. The *South Dakota* was to participate in the San Francisco Navy Day celebration, and it would become Admiral Halsey's flagship. He moved bag and baggage as well as his staff over to this battleship. The *South Dakota* then steamed out of Tokyo Bay for the West Coast.

The following morning at just after 0500, the *Missouri* hoisted anchor and left Tokyo Bay for Guam in company with the destroyer USS *Kimberly* (DD-521). Her role at this huge forward base was to pick up several people who were destined to go back to the United States. It was strange for the ship to travel with its lights blazing, and for the men to be able to smoke out on deck because there was no longer any fear of enemy submarines. But, peace was at hand, even if less than two weeks old.

Another subject that was on the minds of most servicemen was how soon they could be separated from the armed forces and return to their civilian lives. And, what kind of a civilian life would there be? Would jobs, education, and good salaries be available? Was their former profession still in need? Servicemen pondered and discussed these and a thousand other questions. The navy published a magazine, *All Hands,*

Soon after the celebrations of the victory over the Axis, the *Missouri* was called up to deliver the remains of the former Turkish ambassador to Istanbul, Turkey. The battleship and its escort acted as a force to counter Soviet ambitions, which was the primary motive for going to that region. The USS *Power* (DD-839) is to the left of the image, and the Turkish battleship *Yavuz* is to the right of the *Missouri. U.S. Navy*

The *Missouri* anchored at Piraeus, Greece, and its presence was most welcome. The civil war begun by the Communists and inspired by the Soviet Union was substantially affected by the presence of a warship such as the *Missouri*. *U.S. Navy*

that covered many of these concerns, but not all. A point system for the discharge of servicemen had been arranged based on time in service, age, and so forth, but the initial plan was found to be inadequate—everybody wanted out!

The *Missouri* stood into Apra Harbor, Guam, within days after leaving Japan, and picked up a number of veterans whose points entitled them to leave the service. Next stop (without escort) was Pearl Harbor, and she arrived on September 20, 1945. The

Missouri remained for over a week and at one point broke Admiral Nimitz's flag as a show of absolute respect. However, the *Missouri* had an appointment in New York Harbor with President Truman for the Navy Day celebration. There was a stopover at the Norfolk Navy Yard for repairs and the installation of the bronze plaque on the 01 deck identifying the exact location where the surrender was signed. The name of the ship was painted on both sides to help the public identify the vessels as they participated in various ceremonies. Also, it was time for many sailors to disembark and return to their families. But even with the time in Norfolk, the *Missouri* arrived in New York on October 23 and hosted the Trumans on board for the Navy Day celebration on October 27, 1945. This particular date was the birthday of President Theodore Roosevelt, a staunch supporter of the navy, and also one chosen by the Navy League of the United States.

The *Missouri* moored on the west side of the Hudson River among many other famous warships. President Truman violated one navy regulation by allowing the captain's cabin to be officially "wet" for an hour so that hard liquor could be served for the occasion. Unknown to Mr. Truman, there were likely dozens of wet areas aboard a ship the size of the *Missouri*. The crew was wise as wolves when it came to spirits.

On the same day, President Truman was also called upon to participate in the commissioning of a brand-new battle carrier, the USS *Franklin D. Roosevelt* (CVB-42). Its sister ship, the USS *Midway* (CVB-41), is a museum ship in San Diego, California.

The Soviet light cruiser *Sverdlov,* caught by a U.S. Navy surveillance aircraft. As can be seen, the ship looks much like a wartime British or American light cruiser, with a main battery of 6-inch guns yet very little electronics and no missiles. There were to have been twenty-four of this class, yet only fourteen were commissioned in the early 1950s. *U.S. Navy*

One of the duties given junior officers was to escort ranking military officers and their guests around the ship; they seemed to want to visit every nook and cranny of the *Missouri*, including the crew's quarters, which were supposedly off limits. This did provide for some embarrassment during shower periods.

From her decks, President Truman was able to observe the fleet that had defeated the Axis at sea. It was a thrilling time for all New Yorkers to see a victorious navy return to port, even more so since the *Missouri* had been built in New York.

RIGHT President Truman inspects the crew aboard the *Missouri* during his trip back from South America. A chow line was named in his honor, "The Truman Express." *U.S. Navy*

The USS *Missouri* after some modifications to its superstructure, including a more substantial main mast. The seaplanes aft have been replaced by helicopters, which have supplanted almost all of the catapult scout planes. The initial navy helicopter was the HO3S Helo, which, until 1949, had to be temporarily landed on the number-one turret. *U.S. Navy*

Margaret Truman, the president's daughter, eats with the crew of the *Missouri* during her trip with her parents from South America. Later in life, she became a famous author. *U.S. Navy*

After lunch aboard the famous battleship, the Trumans left aboard the destroyer USS *Renshaw* for a continued tour of the ships in the river. A number of luncheons, dinners, and other welcoming events introduced the ships and their crews. Thousands of visitors came aboard the *Missouri* to be a small part of history, and often they decided to take some items away with them—leave their own calling cards. For weeks, the crew cleaned pencil, lipstick, and other markings off the ship in some of the strangest locations. But all good things must come to an end.

The business of ships and fleets was the defense of the nation, and it was time to resume that role. It seemed that the war ended by surrender in Japan was about to take a different form. Trouble was brewing in the Mediterranean, and the *Missouri* was called upon to show her presence.

THE COLD WAR: OVERVIEW

Within a very few months of the formal surrender, some Allies turned into adversaries, and the war that was feared became a reality. What had been thought to be Russian suspiciousness and disdain for the West turned out to be more than true. It was to be the longest war (1946–1991) in the history of the United States and would pit the Western nations against the Soviet Union and the Warsaw Pact. Later, as Communism spread to Asia and Central America, much of the world was again divided into two definable camps bent on world domination and, if need be, world destruction.

At the conclusion of World War II, the United States and the Soviet Union survived as weary but still dominant super powers. The Axis powers were in absolute ruin and would take years to rebuild back to a semblance of definable nations. Even some of the Allies—such as Great Britain, France, and China—lay in economic ruin. Great Britain still depended on assistance from the United States, and would take over five years to regain its stature and ability to feed its people. The United Kingdom would no longer be the British Empire, because the two wars of the twentieth century had virtually bankrupted what had taken centuries to build.

Six years of the most costly war in world history had taken its toll. Over fifty million men, women, and children lost their lives, and the financial costs were prohibitive. Nations that had at one time been preeminent in world politics were barely feeding their populace and the hundreds of thousands of refugees who were crowding every part of free Europe.

Only the United States and Soviet Union were able to maintain a military presence on an international basis, and as expected, victory resulted in the predictable dissolution of their reluctant wartime partnership. Vast differences in core ideologies and beliefs quickly severed the commonality that held these nations in at least a make-believe coalition during the recent world war. Their relationship moved from a desperate alliance characterized by suspicion to one of outright fear. This established the tone for one of the most dangerous periods in world history: the next forty-five years.

The Soviet Union and its satellite nations were determined to eradicate capitalism from the earth. It was quite simple: the United States and her allies had to be destroyed. The world Communist union had to

The *Missouri's* crew celebrates the fourth anniversary of the Japanese surrender on her decks. Turret two is trained as it was on September 2, 1945. *U.S. Navy*

The *Missouri* engages in bombardment practice during a 1949 exercise. It appears that the forward six 16-inch guns have just let loose. *U.S. Navy*

dominate, which meant that first, during the period of 1941 to 1945, the Axis had to be eliminated. But after the surrender was signed aboard the *Missouri*, there was no reason for the two diametrically opposed ideologies to coexist.

Added to this was the desperate economic position that the Soviet Union found itself in as the war drew to a close. The cessation of Lend-Lease and the rejection of Soviet pleas for American loans, coupled with the refusal to allow the Soviets to loot what was left of Germany made a bad situation even worse.

It was obvious to anyone in the diplomatic or military profession that the new superpowers would soon clash. Accordingly, many nations found themselves in one camp or another, and at the midpoint of the twentieth century, this type of war

was a true global war. It had come into focus: a war of ideology, words, minor aggressions, and now escalating expenditures (much on credit) and military hardware growth. This was something new in the annals of warfare. Eventually, it became a war of absolute brinkmanship, and every diplomatic, dishonest, and secretive tool available was employed to win. Four and one half decades forced men, women, and children to live in a nuclear nightmare. Each superpower could destroy civilization many times over, but to what end? Just to maintain latent fear among one's enemies, and maybe find their Achilles' heel.

An American journalist finally defined this novel form of global conflict. Herbert Bayard Swope coined the term "Cold War" in a speech written for Bernard Baruch in 1947, and like Winston Churchill's "iron curtain" reference, these phrases captured the very essence of the war and made it understandable to most of the world. At various times and in various regions throughout the world, the war heated up and threatened to become a hot war.

For the next four and one half decades, the world fully expected that a nuclear or massive conventional war would erupt and consume all of humanity. Each side built and maintained huge, expensive arsenals of weapons. The war took on a life of its own, and eventually evolved into a contest to develop, built, test, and stockpile newer and better weapons for killing all human life. Entire industries were built up and supported by the new arms race. Many of these industries owed their existence to the Cold War and were devastated when it came to an end.

Over the span of two generations, the specter of nuclear war haunted mankind. It periodically escalated to the forefront of world politics yet mainly existed as a backdrop to all ordinary human activity. The Cold War was a near half-century of stress and uneasiness for both sides, and despite redundant system and personal safeguards, the potential for a nuclear strike was ever present.

The Cold War quietly ceased on December 30, 1991, with the formal dissolution of the Soviet Union or, in President Reagan's words, "The Evil Empire." Ironically, the victor at the end of the Cold War was not decided by the amount of potential nuclear mega-tonnage dropped on an opponent, but by the ultimate effect that continued high levels of defense spending had on its national economy. It was won and lost by bean counters!

A three-gun salvo is fired at a North Korean target from the number-two turret. This shelling took place in February 1951, and as the enemy learned again, the *Missouri*'s main battery was formidable. Note the American flag and *Missouri*'s hull number on the turret roof. These weapons could fire up to twenty-five miles, and with a high degree of accuracy. *U.S. Navy*

The *Missouri's* forward 16-inch turret pounds North Korean troops and mechanized equipment that were attacking Hungnam in December 1950. This is a composite image of two negatives taken just minutes apart. *U.S. Navy*

Both adversaries in the Cold War expended huge amounts of money to build and maintain very expensive military hardware. As the years wore on, the high price tag of preparedness progressively sapped the resources of both sides. Change in attitude was inevitable. By the 1980s, most of the Western and Soviet bloc nations had long since reduced their military budgets out of sheer necessity, yet both superpowers maintained a concerted military expansionist pace. Fortunately for mankind, the spending rate could not continue, and by 1990 the entire Soviet system was under siege and rapidly breaking down on a worldwide basis. Within a year, the Cold War came to an end. The United States and the Western nations had triumphed; however, they too were flirting with recessions, double-digit inflation, and near bankruptcy.

The Soviet Union simply imploded and descended into crime and every other related economic and social malady known. The breakup of the Soviet Union and the disintegration of its foundational system have been two of the most significant events in recent world history and will ultimately shape international order far into the twenty-first century.

There is a viable and now probable counterpoint to the end of the Cold War. It has gained some credibility in military and diplomatic circles. While it is true that the Soviet Union is no more and the United States is the dominant superpower, this can change during the space of one generation. After all, Imperial Germany was laid waste at the end of World War I, but scarcely twenty years later was again one of the two top military

The *Missouri* back in Norfolk in 1954 after a hard time off the North Korean coast. Its next assignment will likely be a midshipmen-training cruise. *U.S. Navy*

powers in the world. This time, Germany was willingly in the hands of Nazism, and its national pride was consumed with revenge for the inequity of the Versailles Treaty and the desire for the defeat and subjugation of those that had ransacked their homeland a generation before.

There are those who put forward the argument that World War II, which was instigated by Nazi Germany, was a natural continuation of the crusade begun in August 1914. The twenty-year pause between World War I and World War II was necessary for Germany to rebuild its infrastructure, military, and above all, recover its national dignity. Six years of total war finally caused the defeat of Germany and at the same time pulled down the junior partners in the Axis. It is now again united.

This example of German national resurgence is not an isolated incident in world history, and the possibility exists that Soviet Union could return to its former prominence, perhaps in a different form. The Russian word *peredyshka* captures and synopsizes the method by which this nation could rebuild itself. It translates as the concept of taking time out from world affairs to put domestic, economic, military, and technological affairs in order for the future. It also is a time for acquiring as much technology from all sources (i.e., the West) as is possible, to achieve parity and, ultimately, superiority. Unfortunately, it can also easily be recognized as a natural pause for regrouping for the next round of global aggression. To some, the Cold War is not over, it is just frozen in time and awaiting a thaw. The twenty-first century is

A rare image of the four *Iowa*-class battleships steaming together off the Virginia Capes. It is Battleship Division Two, and the USS *Missouri* is the third ship from the bottom of the image. There are just a very few photos of all of these battleships steaming together. *U.S. Navy*

witnessing the resurgence of Russian nationalism and military power. The current goal is to keep the U.S. Navy at bay.

At the end of World War II, the Soviet Navy was poorly equipped for combat at sea, yet in the decades that followed, it became a navy second only to the U.S. Navy. Had the Soviet system persevered, it is entirely probable that its navy would have become the dominant force at sea. Unluckily for the world, the media is again reporting a resurgence of Russian military power. President Putin is also feeding this nationalistic frenzy.

Although the Cold War at sea was often popularized as a series of standoff incidents between the primary adversaries, it entailed a far greater range of activity. Among the standoff incidents, the most prominent was the 1962 Cuban Missile Crisis. The Cold War at sea encompassed the conflicts fought in Greece, Korea, Vietnam, and the Persian Gulf. No traditional naval battles were ever fought between the principal adversaries during these years, and the war at sea ended as somberly as it began.

In the twenty-first century, the Western navies are in decline, and the Russian Navy is but a shell of its former glory, the Soviet Navy having died an ignoble death. This is the legacy of this war: huge expenditures for combat at sea that never occurred, and now the demise of some of the finest warships ever built long before their time. As was predicted by Lenin, the war could be won in any fashion: militarily, culturally, or economically. Ultimately, the Cold War was won by economics.

THE SOVIET UNION TESTS THE WATERS IN THE MEDITERANEAN

Within a year after the end of World War II, the Soviet Union was demanding possession of the Dodecanese Islands separating the Black Sea from the Mediterranean in order to establish a naval base. The USSR resented the fact that they were bottled up from a naval standpoint, and were prepared to instigate insurgent and guerilla warfare to secure the freedom of the seas.

The United States had vowed that it would contain Communism and the Soviet Union, so the USS *Missouri* and a limited escort was sent to Turkey to return the body of that country's former ambassador.

The demands made by the Soviet Union were to Turkey, and the presence of the *Missouri* in the region in March and April of 1946 had a debilitating effect on Russian power overtures. The next stop was Greece, where the *Missouri* anchored at Piraeus. In both Turkey and Greece, the ship and its crew were welcomed with open arms. Interestingly, the *Missouri* had a far smaller crew than had been required during the war. Most of its antiaircraft guns were no longer manned; thus, a large number of men were superfluous. Ironically, this would be true for the rest of the ship's career. Missiles and electronics would soon replace scores of 20mm Oerlikons and 40mm Bofors AA guns sited in every possible location on deck.

Greece was rife with a violent civil war inspired and funded by the Soviet Union, which would employ any method that might cause a people or nation to embrace the Soviet way. The news media throughout the eastern Mediterranean heralded the warships from America that proved that the West had not abandoned them to the obvious dictatorship of the Kremlin. The *Missouri* and her escort would soon be followed up by a full and permanent fleet—the Sixth Fleet—which would stand toe to toe with the Russians on many occasions.

The Russians had embarked on a warship construction plan that was obsolete at best, but the naval leadership felt that 1,200 submarines split into three defensive rings would protect the motherland. Prewar-designed submarines such as the Shch-II were built for coastal work only, and it was not until the early 1950s that the fifteen-year submarine defensive plan took shape and building began in earnest. The same was true of surface ships. The Red Navy had to retire its hidebound admirals for far-thinking men to begin a surface-ship construction plan. It was not until years later that surface ships entered into their strategic thought processes. They built the *Skory*-class destroyers and the *Sverdlov*-class light cruisers, fourteen of which were built out of the

In a touch of irony, a group of Japanese naval cadets look over the location where the surrender was signed in 1945 on the deck of the *Missouri*. The date is September 7, 1958, over thirteen years later. *Treasure Island Museum*

twenty-four contracted for. Both classes were based on Italian designs that dated back to the mid-1930, and the light cruisers were far less capable that the American *Cleveland*-class light cruisers. It would be a least a decade before the Soviet Navy became a credible blue-water fighting force, and even at that, it would need a quantum leap in technology to catch up to the Western Allies.

The *Missouri's* presence in the Mediterranean gave hope to millions of people who feared that they had been left to their own devices. The sight of this huge warship that represented victory over the Axis was just the tonic that the Greek and Turkish peoples needed to oppose the Soviet Union. The U.S. Navy would maintain a powerful presence in the future of Mediterranean geopolitics.

In late April 1946, the *Missouri* departed for Norfolk, Virginia, via Tangier, Spanish Morocco. Throughout the rest of the 1940s, the *Missouri* made one midshipman cruise after another, and in the summer of 1947, as the only battleship in commission, it journeyed to Rio de Janeiro for a peace conference that included President Truman. The *Missouri* then brought the Truman family back to the United States. Unfortunately, within three years, a hot war would begin when North Korea invaded South Korea. There had been a short period of peace, but it was too good to last, and the Soviet Union and Asian partner China inspired a shooting war that was completely unnecessary. However, it did test the resolve of the West and the newly formed United Nations. The *Missouri* would be in the thick of the war from the outset.

THE KOREAN WAR

The Korean War (or Conflict, or Police Action) has been defined by politicians, soldiers, sailors, and civilians. It all depends on perspective. For those that were being shot at by North Korean bullets from Red Chinese or Russian rifles, it was a war, and for this purpose, it will be treated as a war in this book.

On June 25, 1950, the armed forces of North Korea invaded South Korea with the intention of unifying the country and with the hidden agenda of testing Soviet-backed aggression against the West. A second objective was to determine the support the United States would provide to Japan in the event of a Southeast Asian conflict.

The battleship *Missouri* required an overhaul at the Norfolk Navy Yard after going hard aground at Thimble Shoals on January 17, 1950. She was still the only battleship in commission, so after extensive repairs and reprovisioning, she was posted to Korea. On August 19, 1950, she left Norfolk for familiar waters—Japan. Less than a month later, she was in Kyushu being prepared to support UN forces off the Korean coast. Her first assignment was to bombard Samchok on September 15 as a diversion from the spectacular attack on Inchon. She worked with the heavy cruiser USS *Helena* (CA-75) and two destroyers to assist the Eighth Army and its offensive against the North Korean invaders. Four days later, the battleship was in Inchon and took up duties as a flagship.

She was soon bombarding the coast with her 16-inch guns, and especially the coastal railways that carried much of the enemy's equipment and supplies. Many ships belonged to the "train busters" club, which prided themselves on catching troop and supply trains attempting to make runs to the south. The *Missouri* and many destroyers became quite proficient at hitting these vital targets. In late October 1950, she conducted heavy bombardments of Chonjin, Tanchon, and Wonsan and its harbor.

Hungnam took on a new purpose as it was evacuated by UN troops and many innocent Koreans. The *Missouri* pounded the Hungnam Perimeter to keep the enemy from heavy harassment of UN troops. Finally, they were evacuated, and one of the largest explosions in history devastated what was left of the port area and equipment that could not be transported.

As 1951 began, the war assumed a new face when over one-half million Chinese soldiers began to push the UN forces, which now included troops from sixteen countries, out of Seoul and southward some fifty miles from the thirty-eighth parallel. By March 1951, the United Nations were again in control of Seoul, and the North Koreans had been driven back across the thirty-eighth parallel. For the next two years, the naval war in Korea was one of carrier air strikes, shore bombardments, and fighting Soviet-built aircraft from World War II *Essex*-class carriers that had been refitted to launch and recover jet aircraft. Overall, eleven of these carriers were assigned to the war zone along with the three other *Iowa* class battleships: USS *Iowa* (BB-61), USS *New Jersey* (BB-62), and USS

The *Missouri* had been sitting in mothballs as part of the Bremerton Group of the Pacific Reserve Fleet for eight years when this photo was taken in 1963. This anchorage is located in Puget Sound at Bremerton, Washington. Before being refurbished, she would spend another two decades quietly awaiting a call to arms. Later, the *Missouri* was moored alongside a pier so that visitors could tour the decks. *U.S. Navy*

Wisconsin (BB-64). The *Missouri* had been the first to arrive, and after a number of bombardment strikes and being a major unit in the Cobra patrol, it was time to return to the United States for a complete overhaul. She had already been back to Norfolk for a period of availability in late 1951, but the USS *New Jersey* had arrived to relieve the *Missouri*. The *Missouri* then left for the Norfolk Navy Yard and arrived on May 4, 1952. After a series of midshipmen cruises, the bloodied battleship was assigned to the Bremerton Group of the Pacific Reserve Fleet in Puget Sound, Washington.

After eleven years of hard service, the premier battleship of the U.S. Navy found herself being decommissioned and sealed in mothballs at the sprawling reserve fleet bastion in Puget Sound. All of the most modern techniques for preservation were employed, and it was as if she had rejoined the fleet of World War II. Battleships *Maryland* and *Alabama*, carriers *Bunker Hill* and *Franklin*, dozens of heavy and light cruisers, plus trots of destroyers crowded the anchorage. The *Missouri* was in good company, and many visitors for the Pacific Northwest came to see the most respected battleship ever to grace the oceans. This was to be her home for nearly thirty years.

As to the Korean War, after months of difficult negotiations, the Communists and the United Nations agreed upon and signed an armistice on July 27, 1953. An uneasy peace settled over the region. Six hundred thousand Koreans lost their lives, as well as an estimated one million Chinese. The United Nations lost 55,440 personnel, and of this 94 percent were from the United States. The political and military result of the Korean War was that the United States emerged as a superpower and was destined to lead the free world in its battle to stave off Communist domination. For the U.S. Navy, it was a difficult and different kind of war than the one it had been so successful in just years before. The navy was again appreciated, and it found a definitive role in national defense. The battleship again proved its worth as a coastal bombardment asset, and the *Missouri* had led the way.

The Russian battleship *Potemkin,* pouring smoke from its coal-fired engines, was the infamous site of one of the catalysts of the Russian Revolution in 1905. The officers attempted to feed rotten meat to the crew, and many of the sailors revolted. Battleships were never a mainstay of the Russian Navy, especially after the shameful defeat at the Battle of Tsushima in 1905 by the Japanese Navy. *U.S. Navy*

CHAPTER SIX

A GROWING SOVIET THREAT

FROM THE HEADY DAYS OF THE CZAR and the embarrassing defeat in the Russo-Japanese War (1905), the Russian and later the Soviet Navy declined to almost a nonentity in the international naval community. This was followed by World War I and the Bolshevik Revolution, which took center stage in Russia, and led to the creation of the Soviet Union.

Probably the most famous ship in the Russian Navy at the turn of the century was the battleship *Potemkin.* In 1905, she was the site of a riot, mutiny, and killing over morale, maggoty meat, cruel treatment of seamen, and the absence of equity and decency for the common sailor. The meat being served to the crew was actually crawling with maggots, and the ship's captain, executive officer, and doctor certified that it was safe to eat. The crew then mutinied and killed these three officers and four others. The mutiny spread to a few other ships, but eventually was ended by imperial troops. However, the *Potemkin* became a symbol of the working class forcibly revolting against the upper classes.

The Russian Navy had over three centuries of operations as a forerunner of the Soviet Navy, yet in the twentieth century, it suffered its greatest humiliation. In the turn-of-the-century war between Russia and Japan, the Imperial Japanese Navy destroyed the majority of the czar's fleet during the May 1905 Battle

One of the more colorful posters depicting the riots and mutiny aboard the *Potemkin.* The events aboard this ship served as inspiration to the peasants that had long been treated with disdain by the royalty of the czar. Soon, other ships began to experience mutinies and other forms of silent contempt for naval leadership. *U.S. Navy*

of Tsushima. This particular naval victory earned the Japanese Navy a prominent place in the international community, and at the same time thoroughly disgraced a traditionally powerful European power.

The next opportunity for the Russian Navy to perform was in World War I after being somewhat rebuilt using dreadnought technology. Its performance for the first three years of this war was below mediocre, yet it became infamous for its role during the revolution against the czar in 1917. Various ships and their crews either sided with the Bolshevik revolutionaries or remained loyal to the government in power. Unfortunately, many of the navy's better minds were also purged and murdered if they had been loyal to the previous government. It soon became a peasant navy with little or no formal tradition or skill in naval warfighting.

As to the warships available, there were few operational units, and all were from a former and obsolete era. Many of the shipyards had been severely damaged during the revolution, and the state of the new Soviet Navy in the early 1920s was pitiful. Rebuilding the navy and the merchant fleet was fraught with problems, including a lack of trained labor in the shipyards and related factories. Over the next few years, a series of technologically crude warships were built, including a large number of coastal submarines.

A Soviet missile destroyer in the *Kynda* class harasses an American carrier battle group led by the USS *John F. Kennedy* (CV-67) on October 30, 1969. The incident took place in the Mediterranean, and as can be seen, the USS *Little Rock* (CLG-4) has been placed in between the Soviet destroyer (number 854) and the carrier. This type of behavior at sea became commonplace and dangerous to both navies. *U.S. Navy*

The USS *Kitty Hawk* (CV-63). As of 2007, this is the last of the fossil-fueled aircraft carriers in the U.S. fleet, yet during the Cold War, it was a primary target for all Soviet warships. In 2008, the *Kitty Hawk* will be retired, and the U.S. Navy will have an all-nuclear aircraft carrier force. However, during the Cold War, the basic strategy for the Soviet Navy was to protect the motherland at all costs, and the principal threat was perceived from the American supercarriers. The Soviet Navy literally died when the Russian government collapsed in 1991. However, in 2007, its leaders are again rattling sabers and threatening American carrier battle groups at sea. *U.S. Navy*

World War II came upon the Soviet Union like a thunderclap. Over the four-year period from 1941 to 1945, German forces devastated much of the Soviet Navy, including most of its incomplete construction and the surrounding shipyards. This included the two new thirty-five-thousand-ton battleships. Over half of the surface navy was immobilized or destroyed. Within a few months of the June 1941 invasion, a sustained German air force bombing campaign punished two of the three older battleships as well nearly destroying most of the cruisers in the Black Sea or Baltic fleets. Destroyers fared little better. The performance of the Soviet Navy in World War II was marginal, and most of its losses resulted mostly from mines and bombing attacks.

There were other reasons for the wholesale defeat of the Soviet Navy. Many trained seamen were seconded to the Red Army and its operations as mere cannon fodder. Without hesitation, ship crews were cannibalized for ground operations, and oceangoing

The *Ticonderoga*-class cruiser USS *Yorktown* (CG-48) has just been struck by a Soviet frigate in the Black Sea on February 12, 1988. The Soviet ship is a 1,150-ton-full-load *Mirka*-class frigate generally used for coastal defense and antisubmarine warfare. However, it strayed too close to the *Yorktown* and suffered far more damage than the American warship. *U.S. Navy*

warships were used in the defense of Soviet cities, their heavy guns employed as fixed artillery batteries against advancing German armies. The overall consensus of opinion was that the navy was a second-rate service in the armed forces hierarchy.

Overall, the Soviet Navy was not effective as a surface force and only excelled in supporting ground forces. Its submarine campaign was desultory, and at wars' end, the navy was in a state of complete disarray.

THE SOVIET NAVY IN THE POST–WORLD WAR II ERA

The end of World War II found the Soviet Union with three obsolete battleships. The Royal Navy had loaned the Soviets the HMS *Royal Sovereign*, and it was due to be returned to the United Kingdom when a suitable replacement could be found among the Italian war prizes. The other two (*Gangut* and *Sevastopol*), had been laid down in 1909 and were both coal fired. None of these ships were capable of operations other than minimal coast defense, and due to their obsolescence, they could easily be sunk by aircraft. As surface ships, they were of no value to a modern navy.

On February 3, 1949, under the terms of the Italian Peace Treaty, the Italian battleship *Giulio Cesare* was formally ceded to the Soviet Union as a war prize. She was renamed the *Novorossisk*, and her main battery was re-gunned with Russian 12-inch, .52-caliber barrels. This addition to the Soviet Navy was used extensively for training and trial, and was the last battleship acquired or built by the USSR. The old battleship was accidentally lost while at anchor in the Black Sea on October 29, 1955. She quickly foundered after detonating a World War II German stationary mine. This accident also ended a hidebound naval establishment that was dragging its feet into the modern era of naval tactics and ships. With this came a new face that had an unmistakably positive influence on the future of the Soviet Navy. Admiral of the Fleet of the Soviet Union Sergey Georgyevich Gorshkov. He also ended the battleship experience in the Soviet Navy to come. As to the other classes of warship in the Russian force, in 1956 it was still an eclectic group of ships from virtually every source in Europe. The cruiser force consisted of ex-German, ex-Italian, and ex-American light cruisers and home-built classes dating from World War II and before. All were considered obsolete and almost worthless when compared to most war-built ships in the Western navies.

During the period from 1945 to 1950, the Red Navy had a destroyer inventory of thirteen types. From the lessons learned from other navies and their own growing ability to produce improved warships, the navy began to design a postwar destroyer class that was comparable to those in the West. The first of what would become known as the *Skory* or *Skori* class was built in 1949, and seventy vessels would be commissioned over the next several years. These 3,500-ton, heavily armed ships with speeds up to 38 knots brought international respect to the Soviet Navy, something its leaders craved.

Other destroyers and frigates in the Soviet medium naval forces inventory were older, and a few dated from before the revolution. Most of the frigates and patrol vessels came from foreign sources or had an obvious foreign design influence.

A former Soviet diesel-electric submarine, the *Foxtrot*-class B-39 *Scorpion*. The *Foxtrot* class was one of the better conventionally powered submarines, and at one time, there were sixty-two units in the Soviet Navy. At two thousand tons, the boat had a range of close to twenty thousand miles and was armed with nuclear-tipped torpedoes. This particular boat is located at the San Diego Maritime Museum and is open to the public. During the Cold War, the B-39 sat off the Southern California coast and recorded propeller signatures of the larger American warships. *Author's collection*

To the left is the Soviet nuclear battle cruiser *Kirov* (number 059), which, like its sisters, had been designed to destroy American and NATO aircraft carriers as well as amphibious ships that might threaten Russia. The four *Iowa*-class battleships were brought out of retirement to counter the *Kirov*s. The lead ship, *Kirov,* was laid down in 1973 and completed in 1980. The class had a maximum speed of 32 knots on nuclear power and oil-fired boilers. The primary weapons consisted of SSN-19 Shipwreck missiles, which had the range and explosive power to damage a ship like the *Missouri*. However, the *Missouri* was better armed and more capable of absorbing punishment. The ship to the left is a *Slava*-class heavy cruiser armed with surface-to-surface missiles. At this time, only one of the *Kirov* class is operational, and only for limited periods, due to frequent breakdowns and serious safety violations in its nuclear power plant. *U.S. Navy.*

THE SOVIET NAVY
INITIATES IMPROVEMENTS

The submarine force constituted the bulk of the Soviet Union's naval potential in the initial post–World War II years, and this phenomenon continued throughout much of the forty-six-year Cold War. The influence of late-war German submarine design was unmistakable in the Soviet boats built in the years following the end of the war. In Germany, the Red Army looted and brought back everything remotely related to the undersea warfare. This included the purchase of certain U-boat crews to serve as instructors in the Soviet Navy. The German Type XXI submarine had a definitive influence on Soviet boats for many years.

The primary goal of the Soviet submarine force was to protect the country from attack and invasion by the West, as led by the United States. By 1950, a strategy had been developed and endorsed by the Kremlin. The plan was founded on a fifteen-year submarine-building program that would provide twelve hundred boats of varying capabilities to adequately maintain three defensive rings around the homeland. One hundred small submarines would patrol the inner ring closest to the coastline. Upwards of nine hundred medium-range submarines would patrol the intermediate ring. Two hundred long-range attack boats would patrol the outer ring. The objective of the intermediate and long-range submarines was to sink enemy shipping in the open ocean before it had the opportunity to provide supplies to the attacking and invading forces. This plan was to be in place and operational by 1965. It was fraught with problems and never was accomplished, for a number of obvious reasons. Nuclear power, Western submarine-launched ballistic missiles, and the need to defend Russia from attack from carrier-launched aircraft intervened long before this plan was implemented. However, in the first years after the end of World War II, the Soviet submarine force faced more mundane difficulties.

The submarine force was not standardized, and even by 1950 it consisted of a minimum of sixteen different boat types and different variations of more popular models. A further problem was the lack of trained shipyard workers; competent technicians and dependable shipyard workers were at a premium and difficult to find.

In the years that followed the war, the Red Navy utilized captured boats for operational work and began the design of what would be their most significant immediate postwar submarine class. It was a 1,350-ton, medium-range boat capable of 15 knots submerged and carried six 21-inch torpedo tubes. Code-named the *Whiskey* class, 236 of these medium-range submarines and its many variants were produced. The *Whiskey* class was the largest single class of submarine ever built by any nation, and it was not surprising that many ended up in satellite-state navies. Almost concurrently, the long-range *Zulu* class was built. At 1,950 tons, these boats could range up to twenty thousand miles on their diesel-electric powerplant. Follow-on diesel-electric classes of patrol submarines included the *Romeo* (1958–1961, eighteen boats) and the highly regarded *Foxtrot* (1958–1983, seventy-nine boats). The 2,300-ton (submerged) *Foxtrot* carried ten 21-inch torpedo tubes and had a 19,000-mile range. This boat was the epitome of the conventional submarine and quite popular with other nations. The Russians stopped a planned 160-unit building program at 62 boats in 1971; however, 17 additional units were built for friendly nations.

As to surface ships, the building program was initiated with the mass construction of light cruisers of the *Sverdlov* class and all-gun destroyers of the *Skory* class. Of the planned twenty-four ships in the *Sverdlov* class, fourteen entered fleet service and seventy-five of the eighty planned *Skorys* were commissioned. The *Sverdlovs* mounted twelve 6-inch guns, displaced eighteen thousand tons full load, and could steam at 34 knots. They were handsome ships but were obsolete at birth.

The *Missouri* has been pushed and pulled to the Straits of Juan de Fuca by the smaller tractor tugs from the Bremerton/Seattle area. She left her mooring at the Puget Sound Naval Shipyard, where she had been in mothballs for three decades, and arrived at the gateway to the Pacific Northwest on May 25, 1984. Here, in the straits, she would be bridled to a salvage and rescue tug, the USS *Beaufort* (ATS-2). The *Beaufort* displaced 3,484 tons full load and was powered by diesels that provided six thousand bhp and sufficient power to handle the sixty-thousand-ton battleship. It was a sight that no one ever expected to see—the *Missouri* leaving home after thirty years. However, like her three sisters, she was being towed to a shipyard for modernization. The *Missouri* was on the way to the Long Beach Naval Shipyard. *U.S. Navy*

At this point, the Soviet Navy did not pose any real threat to the West, but after the *Sverdlov* appeared at the 1953 British Coronation Review at Spithead, many naval experts became fearful of the revitalized Soviet Navy. For the next few years, much of Great Britain's naval tactics centered on killing *Sverdlov*s, as if they were of similar caliber to Germany's commerce-raiding *Bismarck*. A major factor in the fascination resulting from the *Sverdlov*s appearance was the overdone cleanliness of the ship and the professionalism of its crew and officers. Many in the West expected a poorly maintained, out-of-date, shoddily built ship manned by undisciplined peasants. The beautiful lines of the *Sverdlov* and the professional behavior of her crew shattered this image. By showing off their finest and most modern heavy warship,

the Soviets accomplished their objective of putting the world on notice that they were in the process of building the finest navy afloat. It was smoke and mirrors. The Soviet Union was building a large navy, but not for offensive operations. The first task was to defend the homeland from attack.

The concern over the Western carrier battle groups was so pervasive in the USSR that various submarine classes were examined for their suitability to carry surface-to-surface guided missiles like Soviet surface ships. Accordingly, several *Whiskey*-class submarines were converted to fire anti-ship cruise missiles.

The first Soviet nuclear powered submarine was the *November* class, which was commissioned in 1958. These 4,800-ton (submerged) boats were capable of diving to 1,650 feet, with a top speed underwater

The battleship has been stripped down with the exception of the main battery and armored areas. Next, the ship will be modernized with new weapons and electronic systems. All of the remaining 40mm quad weapons have been removed as antiques from another era. Overall, the entire process will cost nearly $500 million, as compared to the $100 million expended to build the ship during World War II. *U.S. Navy*

of 25 knots. They were conventionally armed with six 21-inch torpedo tubes, and overall the boats were quite noisy. They were also accident-prone due to poor initial construction and maintenance. The *November* class was followed in 1967 by the much improved *Victor I* class of attack boats. They carried eight 21-inch torpedo tubes and had a top speed of over 30 knots. The lesson learned from the *November* class was applied in the *Victor I* and it became a formidable opponent. The Soviet Navy was not far behind the U.S. Navy in its development of nuclear power for its submarine force and did not abandon diesel-electric technology and building programs.

LEFT The *Missouri* is in dry dock and has just had its hull sandblasted and new anti-fouling paint applied on the underwater surfaces. It is now beginning to look like a brand-new warship. *U.S. Navy*

The big day has arrived for the USS *Missouri* in San Francisco, California. The day was May 10, 1986, and Margaret Truman Daniel was there for the recommissioning, as well as Secretary of Defense Caspar W. Weinberger. A crowd of over ten thousand well-wishers were present to witness the USS *Missouri* come to life and again go to sea to defend the United States. *U.S. Navy*

The *Missouri* at sea after being refurbished and rebuilt. Four months after being recommissioned, the battleship embarked on an around-the-world cruise, stopping at seven nations. The world now was on notice, as was the Soviet Union, that the U.S. Navy had warships that could defeat the best that they could put to sea. *U.S. Navy*

The Soviet Navy began the last twenty years of the Cold War at sea with great promise and instilled fear in the minds of most Western naval professionals. From its rudimentary beginning in the immediate postwar years, it had come a great distance in only a quarter of a century. With its nuclear attack, guided-missile, and ballistic-missile submarines, it quickly posed a real threat to the U.S. and NATO hegemony on the seas. The Russians were not only building what could now

be termed a diverse maritime fighting force of surface ships, submarines, and fast-attack craft, but were also developing shore- and sea-based naval aviation. Naval aviation at sea aboard fixed-wing-aircraft carriers had been considered the dividing line between a superpower navy and one that was second rate. The U.S. Navy obviously dominated in this form of absolute power projection, with Great Britain, France, and other nations playing a comparatively minor role.

The *Missouri* operates with its battle group, which includes cruisers, destroyers, and fleet train support ships (tankers, supply ships, and so forth). This way, the battle group can remain at sea for many weeks and be prepared for any contingency. *U.S. Navy*

SOVIET NAVAL METHODS OF CHALLENGING THE U.S. NAVY AT SEA

As soon as the Soviet Navy began to sail in blue waters beginning in the Mediterranean, its ships and submarines began a program of interfering with U.S. and NATO naval operations. This took the form of ramming American warships and bumping submarines with their own nuclear boats. Additionally, their surface ships interfered with flight operations of Western aircraft carriers. Soviet cruisers and destroyers would cross dangerously close off the bows of aircraft carriers that were launching or recovering aircraft and often caused a suspension of operations until they could be driven off.

This began in the late 1960s and continued through the 1980s, despite a formal treaty signed on May 25, 1972, entitled the Incidents at Sea Agreement. Even with all of the pomp and ceremony as the treaty was signed in Moscow, it was not long before the Soviet Navy resumed its practices of harassing American and NATO ships. During the 1960s alone, there were nine incidents where Soviet submarines collided with American warships. Eventually, as the Soviet Navy began to wax and wane, the incidents stopped. However, a six-hundred-ship U.S. Navy had some influence on Soviet at-sea behavior. To combat the U.S. Navy's larger warships, the Soviets began to build nuclear battle cruisers: the *Kirov* class.

A NEW THREAT EMERGES: THE KIROV-CLASS BATTLE CRUISER

The Soviet surface fleet stunned the world in 1980 when Western observers first saw the guided-missile battle cruiser *Kirov*. This class proved that Soviet naval intent was to move from home waters and operate on a worldwide basis. Of course, the defense of mother Russia was not forgotten, and in a 1985 exercise, a surface-attack group led by the *Kirov* demonstrated how this type of force would defeat a hostile Western battle group.

The first nuclear-powered surface ship in the Soviet Navy was also the largest ship they had built to date, at 24,300 tons full load and 814 feet in length. Although primarily powered by nuclear reactor, the *Kirov*s also utilized a fossil-fuel backup system. The *Kirov* class was to have five ships, yet only four were built. They were armed (or, perhaps, over-armed) with a variety of sophisticated and diverse weapons that included SSN-19 cruise missiles, SAN-6 and SAN-4 surface-to-air missile launchers, guns, torpedoes, anti-submarine warfare (ASW) rocket launchers, and helicopters for ASW and anti-ship missile guidance. The SSN-19 had a three-hundred-mile range, and there were twenty angled vertical-launch tubes in the forecastle. This missile could be armed with a nuclear or high-explosive warhead. Ultimately, this type of system was destined replace the single- and twin-arm missile launchers that served most navies for the major part of the Cold War.

Other guided-missile cruisers built by the Russians during the final years of the Cold War included the *Slava, Kresta II,* and *Kara* classes. All were armed with anti-ship and surface-to-air missiles. In particular, the *Slava* class boasted sixteen SSN-12 anti-ship launch tubes that crowded her amidships main deck. The *Slava*s looked menacing and were designed to attack intruding American aircraft carriers.

The forward main battery of 16-inch, .50-caliber guns opens fire on targets up to twenty-four miles distant. The shells were guided by a Mk 38 main battery director, which had not been modified materially since World War II. It was "if it is not broken, do not fix it," and it was not broken and worked quite well. Once the director was on target, the main guns could hit the target within one hundred meters continuously. Crew were forbidden to be close to the barrels or turrets when shooting was taking place, as it could deafen them permanently and even blow them over the side of the ship. The concussion from the explosion of five powder bags and a two-thousand-pound shell coming out of one of the gun barrels was a sound and experience unlike any other. *U.S. Navy*

On many occasions, gunner's mates have used specialized ramming rods with sponges on the ends in order to clean the barrels of artillery or naval guns. In the case of the *Missouri* and its nine 16-inch, .50-caliber barrels, something more sophisticated was needed. The device shown here was developed, and it is the barrel cleaner for the 16-inch gun, which had to reach some 60 inches into the barrel. An unpolished or filthy, un-oiled barrel could create a safety hazard for the gun crew and at the same time, have a negative affect on the gun's accuracy. This drum-like item is the brush that was used to clean and polish the barrel interior. Typically, aboard the *Iowa*-class battleships, there was a seventy-seven-man crew per turret to perform all of the functions required to maintain and fire the guns. *U.S. Navy*

THE U.S. NAVY CHECKMATES THE SOVIET NAVY

As World War II ended, it became clear that the Soviet Union would soon become an adversary rather than a reluctant and rude ally. The USSR had a wholly different agenda now that the Axis had been defeated, and this included the spread of Marxism Leninism throughout the world by any means possible. The Soviets made attempts to achieve this goal in Europe, the Mediterranean, Africa, South America, and, of course, Asia. There were some successes, yet the failures were greater. At the same time, it was becoming obvious that the Soviet Union would require a blue-water navy to carry its message from the homeland. They found this out most graphically in October 1962.

The Soviet hierarchy had decided to place short- and medium-range nuclear-tipped ballistic missiles on Cuban soil as a counterpoint to a suspected planned U.S. invasion. The United States had planned no such invasion after the disastrous failure of the Bay of Pigs attack, but the Cuban government convinced a very willing Soviet government to bring in portable missile launchers and missiles. Unfortunately, the United States had a very powerful navy, and the Soviet Union was able to deploy a mere three *Foxtrot*-class conventional submarines to protect the merchant ships transporting the missiles. On the other hand, the U.S. Navy deployed fifty-two surface ships within three days of discovering the missiles, and within ten days, there were 115 destroyers, two modern cruisers, and two supercarriers to provide air cover, including nuclear weapons. In short, the Soviet Union was outclassed and had to back down or risk all-out war. They withdrew but learned the disadvantage of not having a blue-water navy.

As the years wore on, and the USSR and the United States were involved in brushfire wars, it soon became evident that these two nations were to be the world's new superpowers. To fulfill this role, the Soviet Union was compelled to catch up to the United States in any and all arms races.

For all intents and purposes, the four battleships of the *Iowa* class had been put to bed permanently, with the exception of the USS *New Jersey,* which was refitted for one short tour in the Vietnam War in 1969. However, the Soviet Union's primary tactic at sea was to protect the motherland by destroying any amphibious invasions and sinking the supercarriers that might threaten air attacks. To accomplish this, the Soviets would arm almost every surface ship with anti-ship missiles and fit many submarines with guided missiles. The warfighting philosophy was simple and direct: fire everything available at the target. In other words, the Soviet surface force was a "one-shot navy" destined to sink American and NATO centerpiece warships. The primary prizes were the supercarriers and the large amphibious ships.

The one ship type that was not in the Soviet inventory was a large battle cruiser that could deal punishment and survive attacks by U.S. and NATO surface ships. The ship design selected was that of the *Kirov.* This was the incredible battle cruiser that was partially driven by nuclear power and armed to the teeth with anti-ship missiles, including vertical launching system (VLS) silos.

Without building an entirely new class of warship, the U.S. Navy decided to activate all four of the *Iowa*-class battleships as a countermeasure to the *Kirov* class. At first, many in the Pentagon felt the Navy Department had gone mad and could not believe that four ancient battleships designed in the 1930s would be called out of retirement to fight again. After all, the *Missouri* had been resting for nearly thirty years with such luminaries as the USS *Maryland* (BB-45), USS *Indiana* (BB-59), USS *West Virginia* (BB-48), USS *Colorado* (BB-46), and dozens of other famous and obscure ships.

Many in the media and Congress shared this incredulity of reactivating a throwback to another age, but not the president, Ronald Reagan. Consequently, the *Missouri* received the call in early 1984 to be towed to the Long Beach Naval Shipyard for a complete overhaul and modernization. This was to be no ordinary upgrade and paint job. Fortunately, the staff at the Naval Inactive Ships Maintenance Facility had taken excellent care of the *Missouri* as well as her three sisters, *New Jersey, Wisconsin,* and *Iowa.* As an aside, years before, President Truman had chastised President Eisenhower for placing the *Missouri* in Bremerton, Washington, as if to banish the great ship. He felt that the battleship should be in New York Harbor for the world to see. On the other hand, thousands of people visited the *Missouri* during her three-decade stay in Puget Sound, including the author.

On May 14, with towing bridle in place, the *Missouri* was warped away from its pier, which it

This secondary battery of 5-inch, .38-caliber guns in a twin barrel mount was one of three mounts per side after the 1980s rebuild of the *Iowa*-class battleships. The 5-inch guns were controlled by a Mk 37 gun director, of which there were four units aboard the *Missouri.* These mounts could fire up to twenty rounds per minute per barrel, yet the 130-degree heat in the tropics quickly reduced that number due to crew exhaustion. The shell weighed fifty-four pounds, and combined with the Mk 37 director and the more than eighteen-thousand-yard range, the accuracy level was phenomenal. Of course, this was due to the human element as much as the electronic aids. Also shown on the port side is a mock up of the Harpoon missile canisters, and to the right is a Tomahawk missile with its stub wings deployed. Just aft of funnel number two is the Mk 37 gun director for the number-three 16-inch turret aft. *Author's collection*

had shared with the older cruisers USS *Oklahoma* (CG-5) and USS *Chicago* (CG-11). The USS *Beaufort* (ATS-2), a salvage and rescue tug, was chosen to tow the 60,000-ton ship to its new base in Southern California. The trip took eleven days, and the cost to refit her would top $480 million, or approximately five times her original construction expense.

UPGRADED TO FIGHT THE KIROV CLASS

The *Missouri* was placed in dry dock at the Long Beach Naval Shipyard and work began immediately by stripping out everything that would not fit with 1980s technology. As an example, low-wattage light bulbs in many compartments were immediately replaced by high-intensity lighting.

One of the four 20mm Phalanx CIWS (close-in weapon system) aboard the *Missouri*. All had a 360-degree coverage, and when set on automatic, would fire on *any* incoming aircraft, missile, shell, or bomb. It had no IFF (identification, friend or foe) to segregate friendly from enemy aircraft in the early days of this weapon system. It fired up to three thousand rounds of depleted uranium (the densest substance then available) per minute and had an 80 percent hit rate. *Author's collection*

The *Missouri* would be rebuilt along the lines of the USS *Iowa*, as she had not been upgraded like the USS *New Jersey*. Much had to be done to the ship to accommodate the new weapons that were being installed, along with the electronic packages to operate them.

The *Missouri* was to retain her nine 16-inch, .50-caliber Mk 50 main battery of nine barrels in three triple mounts. Each gun was capable of firing an armor-piercing round 41,600 yards, or approximately twenty-five miles. A nine-shell salvo of either high explosive (HE) or armor-piercing (AP)

Armored box launcher (ABL) for the BGM-109 Tomahawk missile. This particular ABL contains Tomahawk numbers one, two, three, and four, and is on the forward deck on the starboard side of the *Missouri*. When the missiles were to be fired, the armored box cover would be lifted and the missile exposed to be fired. A booster propelled the Tomahawk ten miles before a cruise turbofan was initiated. The *Missouri* carried thirty-two Tomahawk missiles of various types and provided the long-range strike capability. *Author's collection*

Chaff launchers on the starboard side of the *Missouri*. This was one of eight Mark 137 SRBOC launchers (super-rapid-blooming off-board chaff). This chaff would deploy and resemble the *Missouri,* and hopefully deceive enemy missiles. These were part of the ship's last-ditch defensive measures. *Author's collection*

projectiles could be fired at the rate of two per minute with exceptional accuracy. This weapon could fire one of twelve different projectiles, depending on the mission profile, and its AP shells could penetrate twenty-two inches of armor, depending on the angle of the shell hit. The destructive power of the 2,700-pound AP or 2,000-pound HE shell was unimaginable. The projectiles were fired through the use of sewn powder bags containing explosive nitrocellulose pellets. When rebuilding the four *Iowa*-class battleships, it became necessary to replace the powder bags, as the propellant does deteriorate over time. (One other planned shell was a subcaliber extended-range projectile of 1,000 pounds that could have reached some seventy thousand yards, or nearly thirty-eight miles, but this project did not come to be.)

A telephone in the *Missouri's* captain's cabin circa World War II. It still is functional but is wholly different from twenty-first-century communications equipment. *Author's collection*

During World War II, there was a need for a large number of barrage-type secondary batteries; however, in the 1980s, space was required for missiles and other contemporary weapons to counter modern threats. The *Missouri* was reduced from ten 5-inch mounts to six, or, three twin-gun mounts on each side as opposed to the original five per side. This represented a reduction from twenty 5-inch guns to twelve. The 5-inch, .38-caliber gun could fire one of ten types of projectile, depending on the need. The shells generally weighed fifty-four pounds using a fifteen-pound powder charge, and had a range of 18,200 yards. The maximum elevation of the guns was eighty-five degrees. Some of the varieties had VT proximity fuses (with a self-contained radio transmitter and receiver) to explode the shell near the incoming enemy aircraft. A good gunnery crew could fire twenty-two rounds per barrel per minute. However, the heat and noise was horrendous in the 5-inch mount. This rate of fire was for limited times only, as exhaustion would quickly set in on the gun crew.

A crew cafeteria-style mess entitled the "Missouri Express" was one of the more popular places to eat, especially during working hours or during times when the ship might be called upon to go into action. The food aboard the *Missouri* was above average, as was testified to by the seagulls that followed the ship to its anchorages. *Author's collection*

The 20mm Vulcan CIWS (close-in weapon system) replaced the scores of 1940s-era 20mm Oerlikon and 40mm Bofors guns employed as antiaircraft weaponry. The large numbers of 20mm and 40mm guns mounted all over the ship in any vacant space was in response to the Japanese kamikaze threat. The changeover to the four Mk 15 CIWS weapons provided the *Missouri* with a form of six-barreled Gatling gun that could fire up to three thousand rounds of depleted uranium (now titanium is used) per minute. The weapon's precursor was the U.S. Air Force's M61 Vulcan gun. The originally designed kill range was two thousand yards and was radar directed. All four weapons were high up on the superstructure of the *Missouri* and could be set on automatic to destroy any selected incoming threat. The navy made claims that this weapon could shoot down an incoming .30-caliber bullet, but most battleship captains were satisfied if it prevented a missile from hitting the ship! The original CIWS did not have IFF (identification, friend or foe) when set on automatic. The system merely assumed any incoming threat had to be destroyed. This was remedied in future system

The *Missouri* made the first around-the-world voyage by an American battleship since the turn-of-the-century days of the Great White Fleet initiated by President Theodore Roosevelt. Here the ship is moored in Sydney Harbor and being reviewed by none other than Prince Philip of the British royal family. The *Missouri* visited seven counties,and the visitors to the ship were in awe of this now modern battleship. It gave hope to our allies and fear to our enemies. *Author's collection*

The *Missouri* enters Pearl Harbor and renders honors to the USS *Arizona* Memorial, seen off the bow of the battleship in the late 1980s. From that time forward, the *Missouri* had two major battles to fight before returning to Pearl Harbor as a memorial ship. Iran was threatening war, openly attacking supertankers coming to and from Kuwait. The Iranian Navy was using Swedish Boghammar cigarette-type high-speed boats armed with missiles to attack the tankers by hitting the ships' bridge structures. Soon, of greater significance was the spontaneous invasion of Kuwait by its neighbor, Iraq. The government of Iraq had defaulted on billions in loans to sustain their fight with Iran, and what better way to avoid repayment but to conquer your lender. Paradoxically, the United States traditionally had backed Iraq. *U.S. Navy*

upgrades. Since the 1980s, the weapon has been vastly improved and in some cases completely replaced by the Rolling Airframe Missile (RAM).

There were a small number of .50-caliber machine guns for close defense against suicide boats or swimmers, and of course there was an armory for other small arms.

The systems that took a quantum leap in updating the *Missouri* and her three *Iowa*-class sisters were the Harpoon and Tomahawk missile systems, which were the great equalizers when combating any Soviet warship or battle group. Not only could the *Missouri* respond accurately and rapidly, but she could take a tremendous amount of punishment and still remain in the fight. That was something that the Soviet *Kirov* class was incapable of doing.

The Tomahawk was and is a cruise missile that in the mid-1980s gave the battleships their long-distance strike capability. The *Missouri* carried eight Mk 143 armored box launchers (ABL) in which thirty-two BGM-109-series Tomahawks were housed. They could be fired from the ABL, which could be elevated to a firing position. In the 1980s, the Tomahawk cruise missile was not nearly as sophisticated as it is in the early twenty-first century. There were three basic variants: TLAM-C land attack (700-nautical-mile range); TLAM-N with a nuclear tipped warhead (1,500-nautical-mile range); and the TASM anti-ship version (250-nautical-mile range). After the missile is fired, its booster takes it eleven miles from the ship. Then, small wings deploy, converting the missile into a small-aircraft-like vehicle, and an onboard turbofan engine propels the Tomahawk for the rest of the distance of up to 2,643 miles to target with a 510-pound conventional warhead. The Tomahawk was either guided by pre-planned contour matching or radar.

The RGM-84 Harpoon was the *Missouri*'s anti-ship missile that could disable all but the most heavily armored ships. The Harpoon was housed in Kevlar armored canisters. There were sixteen missiles in four quad Mk 141 launching cells that had an eighty-five- or sixty-four-mile range, depending on the warhead selected. The Harpoon batteries were mounted amidships, with two quads on port and starboard. The missile batteries brought the four *Iowa*-class battleships into the modern age, and

The Persian Gulf was not the only seat of world unrest. Unknown to even the most astute espionage agents, in 1989 the Soviet Union was about to collapse. Its warships spent far less time at sea, and saber rattling had diminished. Internal problems were tearing the nation apart, and finally, the entire system of government imploded and collapsed. Here, two of its destroyers had sunk at their moorings, and although they were slated for scrapping, now they and other ships were simply left without any monitoring. Unfortunately, this also included the older nuclear submarines, which still had missiles, mines, and torpedoes aboard, yet had been abandoned in the backwaters of various ports. *Author's collection*

truly made them the most powerful warships afloat. The Soviet *Kirov* was absolutely no match for these warships. They had been checkmated.

For defensive measures, the *Missouri* had electronic countermeasures (ECM). The threat-warning system, consisting of the AN/SLQ-32V, could jam and deceive any incoming attackers. In addition, the *Missouri* and its sisters had eight Mk 137 SRBOC (super-rapid-blooming off-board chaff) launchers. These could send up a radar likeness of the *Missouri* that was meant to deceive incoming radar-directed missiles. In addition, the *Missouri* was equipped with a SLQ 25 NIXIE, a towed device to confuse enemy torpedoes.

The entire process to rebuild the *Missouri* to 1980s standards began when the ship left the Inactive Ships Maintenance Facility in Bremerton, Washington, on May 14, 1984. Her destination was the Long Beach Naval Shipyard, and on May 10, 1986, she was recommissioned in San Francisco, California. Margaret Truman Daniel rechristened the great ship, as she had done before in World War II. The *Missouri* was then ready to face anything the Soviet Navy had to offer.

THE RAPID DECLINE OF THE SOVIET NAVY

It was less than five years later that the Soviet Union literally imploded as a government and overall system. Thus, the Cold War at sea for the Soviet Union ended with the dissolution of its government in 1991, yet for the navy the dissolution had begun in the late 1980s. The fleets, including nuclear-powered ballistic missile submarines and attack submarines, began to spend more time in harbor or undergoing sporadic maintenance. Funding availability and the infrastructure to support a world-class navy began to decline, and the overall threat of war at sea ended. Western weapons, electronic marvels, and ship sizes and numbers did not conquer the Soviet Navy: it was internal economics and social change. The once proud and growing navy that Admiral Gorshkov had dreamed of began to die soon after his retirement in 1985, and was but a shadow of its former self by 1991. The recommissioning of the four *Iowa*-class battleships may have had something to do with the major change in world events.

On March 27, 2006, the Russian Federated Navy (RFN) destroyer *Marshal Shaposhnikov* (number 543) slowly makes its way into Agana Harbor and to the American Naval Base in the Territory of Guam. The *Udaloy*-class destroyer was one of four ships joining the U.S. Navy in an operation dubbed Passex. The Russian ship is reasonably modern, as are the *Sovremennyy*-class destroyers that are the backbone of the Russian destroyer force. *U.S. Navy*

Operation Earnest Will in action, with a fully laden re-flagged supertanker under the guard of the U.S. Navy. The frigate ahead of the tanker is the *Oliver Hazard Perry*-class fast missile frigate USS *Hawes* (FFG-53). Its bow identification numbers have been painted a dark gray, as were most of the one hundred U.S. Naval vessels operating in the Gulf. This was thought to confuse the enemy. The battleships also acted as escorts. *U.S. Navy*

CHAPTER SEVEN

NEAR-EAST INTERESTS

ASIDE FROM SAND, THE NEAR EAST HOLDS the world's greatest crude oil reserves, and Western nations led by the United States have been a routine customer for decades, primarily since World War II. The local peoples generally had divided the region into kingdoms—fiefdoms and governments that originated from desert tribes dating back to the pharaohs. However, since World War II and the rapid growth in worldwide demand for oil, leaderships of all types in this region now know the value of a petrodollar and also know that they can control much of the world's energy and economic systems. At one time in the not-too-distant past, crude oil was selling for less than ten U.S. dollars per barrel, and in late 2007 the going price had topped ninety-five dollars. This makes for interested investors and others who might just seize the product rather than pay the high prices.

In essence, that is what Iraqi dictator Saddam Hussein did in 1990. From 1980 to 1988, Iraq had fought a long, expensive, and bloody war with its neighbor, Iran, on credit extended by another neighbor, Kuwait. There was also some question as to whether Kuwait was the legitimate property of Iraq as well. Iraq had long believed that Kuwait was simply another state within Iraq and was certainly not an independent nation. The best way to solidify this was to invade and conquer the little kingdom, and there

A Chinese-manufactured Silkworm missile. The Iraqis fired these crude but heavily armed missiles at the *Missouri* in the latter days of the war, and a British warship, the HMS *Gloucester*, fired two Sea Dart antiaircraft missiles at the threat. One missed, yet the other splashed the Silkworm before it hit any shipping off the coast of Kuwait. *U.S. Navy*

The *Missouri* launches a Tomahawk missile at a target in Iraq. The booster rocket took the missiles eleven miles from the ship, and then its turbofan engine cut in, and it was on its way to the target. The Tomahawk missile of the late 1980s had been substantially improved over the last several years, and its capability and accuracy was unquestionable. *U.S. Navy*

was no expectation that the United States or the United Nations would do much more than lodge a protest. Accordingly, in the summer of 1990, Iraqi armed forces invaded the tiny but very wealthy kingdom to "protect" it and, at the same time, discharge Iraq's entire multi-billion-dollar war debt. Within weeks, a military coalition led by the United States launched Operation Desert Shield, a buildup of army, navy, and air force assets in the region from a large number of nations. At the outset of 1991, Desert Shield was a massive military machine aimed right at Iraq, with the objectives of evicting Iraqi forces from Kuwait and restoring its sovereignty. The actual attack by air, sea, and ground forces of the coalition converted Desert Shield to Desert Storm. Within days, the Iraqi ground forces were escaping from Kuwait in any way possible, and what was once one of the largest armies in the

world had been reduced substantially. Aside from the overall rout of the Iraqi Army, Operation Desert Storm showed the world what technology had been achieving since the Vietnam War, including smart bombs, highly accurate Tomahawk cruise missiles, and stealth fighters and bombers that penetrated Iraqi air defenses without being identified. It seemed that every aspect of the war as fought by the U.S.-led coalition was far superior to what the enemy put forward on the battlefield.

Even the 16-inch and 5-inch shells that were rained down from the *Iowa*-class battleships such as the *Missouri* on Iraqi military targets in Kuwait were terrifying to the much-vaunted Republican Guard (the best of the best in the Iraqi Army). The *Missouri* also launched a number of Tomahawk cruise missiles that sought out their targets and quickly obliterated them.

However, the story of what became known as the Gulf War (1990–1991) began in the year following the end of World War II—1946—and, ironically, the USS *Missouri* was involved in a peripheral way at that time.

SOVIET INTEREST IN THE MIDDLE EAST

As World War II came to an end, the Soviet Union, and in particular, Joseph Stalin, cast covetous eyes on the Middle East. Stalin had already become militarily and ideologically involved with Turkey and Greece in the eastern Mediterranean, and the United States very nearly dispatched a large aircraft carrier air group plus cruisers, destroyers, and a fleet-support unit to maintain a long-term presence.

The diplomats in Washington, D.C., felt that this was too much for the Soviet government to stand for without some form of retaliation. Consequently, the USS *Missouri*, USS *Providence* (CL-82), and USS *Power* (DD-839) brought back the body of the former ambassador from Turkey to his home country. The ships anchored in Istanbul Harbor from April 5–9, 1946. Aside from carrying out a proper diplomatic mission, the *Missouri* and its samll task force conveyed the power of the United States and that it would stand behind Turkey and Greece. If Communist insurgents were attempting to overthrow the governments of these democracies, which were also pro-Western, then the military might of America could be brought to bear.

The remotely piloted vehicle (RPV) is safely caught in the mesh on the stern of an *Iowa*-class battleship. The space available on the fantail was not sufficient for a conventional landing, so trapping the RPV in the netting was the next best alternative. *U.S. Navy*

Interestingly, the Soviet Union read this message to include more than two nations bordering on the Mediterranean. It also meant that the United States was prepared to flex its military muscles if the Soviet Union intervened in the Mediterranean or the Middle East.

Two years later, Secretary of the Navy James Forrestal warned the administration that a third world war would cause the United States to be short of at least two million barrels of crude oil each day. Although the United States was generating 62 percent of its requirements for crude oil in 1948, the Middle East was exporting 12 percent of the world's need. Seven years later, in 1955, the Gulf region was providing 20 percent of the world's needs in crude oil, and the United States had dropped to supplying 43 percent of its own needs. Forrestal was correct in his assumption that the United States had to exercise a degree of control of Middle East oil and prevent the Soviet Union from becoming preeminent in the region. This required exercising a high degree of diplomacy and understanding and appreciating Middle Eastern politics, religion, and culture. It also demanded having a military presence that was appreciated and impressive in the Persian Gulf.

The reasons that made Middle Eastern oil attractive were:

- Refinery capacity in the region had been greatly expanded during World War II; thus, petroleum products could be made and shipped at the point of origin.

On January 12, 1991, an Iraqi sea mine drifts behind the *Missouri* in the Persian Gulf. The ship's EOD Team would soon dispose of it. The sea mines, which were mainly of local construction or from the ex-Soviet Union, posed a real threat to coalition shipping. *U.S. Navy*

The USS *Missouri* leads a surface action group, or SAG. While not as far-ranging as an aircraft carrier battle group, the surface action group was a valuable adjunct to the navy in the 1980s, with the threat of the Soviet Navy. The Soviet Navy had begun building the *Kirov*-class nuclear battle cruisers, and the only American warships that could effectively challenge them in a sea fight were the *Iowa*s and their surface action groups. *U.S. Navy*

- Having Persian Gulf reserves would forestall American domestic shortages and allow for stockpiling oil within the United States. At end of the Second World War, Americans were anxious to own automobiles again (the single greatest user of gasoline). They would remember shortages at the voting booths, and wary politicians anxious to retain their positions in government would be cautious in this area.
- Middle Eastern oil products were less expensive on balance to the American consumer. Domestic gasoline was still twenty-four cents per gallon as late as 1966.
- The proximity of navy fuel and aviation gasoline refined in the Middle East to the operating areas of the U.S. Navy (Mediterranean and Pacific) made it much less expensive.

Overall, the Soviet Union did not have a direct effect on Middle Eastern politics, yet it was instrumental in selling arms to its dictators and royal families. As to the United States, it ultimately created a Middle East Task Force, which grew from a single, lightly armed warship to aircraft carrier battle groups of a nuclear carrier, along with Aegis cruisers and destroyers as well as fast frigates. And with the Iraqi invasion of Kuwait in 1990, American battleships were also called upon to join the ever growing force of international navies.

In the 1980s, the presence of potentially hostile American ships caused Iran to step up its attacks on shipping as it passed through the Strait of Hormuz, with special emphasis on Kuwaiti tankers. The "Tanker Wars" were about to escalate, with the U.S.-led Western powers at the center. However, long before there was

The *Missouri* fires all three turrets at targets near Hawaii to hone the skills of the main-battery staff. The roar of these weapons will never be forgotten by those who were close. To most naval personnel, the firing of a 16-inch weapon was quite a thrill. *U.S. Navy*

such a strong American naval presence, both Iraq and Iran began to attack merchant ships with an emphasis on oil tankers in order to shatter the other's economic stability. This tactic began in 1980 with the beginning of the Iran-Iraq War.

THE POLITICAL CONTEXT CHANGES IN THE MIDDLE EAST

However, there were other issues that had become apparent from 1950 to 1980. Much of them centered on Arab nationalism, which was on the rise, and countries with petrodollars found themselves with growing international importance. And, these oil-rich nations were being courted by arms dealers who could sell them the latest in military hardware. Local skirmishes had been common for centuries. Now, with weapons of mass destruction, long, drawn out wars became the norm, with catastrophic results.

The war between Iran and Iraq, which began in 1980 and lasted through 1988, seemed to dominate much of the activity in the region during this period and engulfed other nations as well. The Iran-Iraq War was a violent, no-holds-barred conflict that resulted in the deaths of millions of military and civilian personnel. It was fought with a combination of U.S. and Soviet equipment as well as tactics taught by advisers from the nations who were selling the products. As the war escalated, the United States found itself in the position of supporting not only Iraq but Iran as well. Iran's F-14 Tomcats were more than a match for the Iraqi Air Force, and rather than engaging the Tomcats, Iraqi fighter jets would simply turn and run.

The Iraqi Air Force did realize one stunning victory, and that was on the morning of May 17, 1987. The American missile frigate USS *Stark* (FFG-31) was on patrol, and an Iraqi Mirage F-1 fighter-bomber released two French-made Exocet missiles at the frigate. The 20mm CIWS was in standby mode; the Mk 36 SRBOC chaff countermeasure systems were not armed, and the missiles came at the ship in a blind spot out of the view of the STIR (separate target illumination radar). Thus, the only item seen by a lookout was a thin smoke trail from the Exocet that was incoming at almost water level. Both missiles struck the unwary ship and nearly sank her. Thirty-seven crewmen were killed and several seriously injured. The *Stark* survived the attack through effective damage

control and was able to get to Bahrain on its own power. The lesson from this unwarranted attack by a supposed friend was that war in the Persian Gulf knows no friends. Additionally, treaties and protocols mean very little to people who have been fighting over timeless issues that the Western mind cannot appreciate. Iraq apologized profusely, and it claimed that the Mirage pilot was executed, but thirty-seven men were dead and millions in taxpayer dollars had been wasted.

Neither Iraq nor Iran was naval minded, and they concentrated on the ground and air war. However, both countries did utilize inexpensive floating mines, especially in a narrow chokepoint in the Strait of Hormuz. Most of the shipping consisted of local cargo ships traveling among the ports in the Persian Gulf, and of course, a few naval vessels from the United States and nations bordering the Gulf. The sea mines took a drastic toll among commercial ships, such as the 415,000-ton tanker *Bridgewater,* and tankers carrying petroleum products from Kuwait seemed to be targeted not only by mines, but by Iran's small, high-speed Boghammar patrol boats.

Another favorite weapon of the Iranian military was the Chinese-built Silkworm missile. It was somewhat of a crude, unsophisticated missile that had a range of fifty-nine miles and a 1,131-pound warhead. It was not very accurate, but the size of the warhead did substantial damage if it hit anywhere near the target. China finally agreed to stop exporting the missile in 1988.

The Boghammar was capable of carrying surface-to-surface missiles, which the Iranians seemed to aim at the bridges of the supertankers to destroy the command-and-control capability. Iran had nearly fifty of these very-high-speed, cigarette-type craft that more than made up for a lack of more substantial warships. Although they did have two frigates, these and over half of the Iranian Navy were destroyed after the frigate USS *Samuel B. Roberts* (FFG-58) was nearly sunk by an Iranian sea mine on April 14, 1988. The U.S. Navy retaliated by initiating Operation Praying Mantis, which called for the immediate destruction of two oil platforms and a frigate. Foolishly, the Iranian Navy attempted a counterattack, which brought the wrath of the U.S. Navy down upon their forces, and most of their operational ships were destroyed. A week later, the U.S. Navy also stated that it would come to the aid of any ship being harassed or under attack by any Iranian forces outside the exclusion zone. This was entitled "distress assistance," and really meant that the U.S. Navy would engage any Iranian warship or aircraft threatening friendly or neutral shipping.

Kuwait approached the United States for relief from attacks primarily by Iran on its shipping in the Gulf. They suggested that the U.S. Coast Guard escort vessels in the Gulf and protect them against Iranian patrol boats, mines, and Silkworm missiles. An operation entitled Earnest Will was initiated and began with re-flagging eleven Kuwaiti ships with the American flag. Operation Earnest Will was later formally inaugurated to re-flag neutral (primarily Kuwaiti) tankers and merchant ships with the flag of the United States. Thus, an attack on them by Iran would be the same as a warlike act against the United States. Firm and open support for this action came from France, the United Kingdom, Italy, Belgium, and the Netherlands. This enraged Iran, who threatened that the seas would run red with the blood of Americans due to their interference. Overall there were 127 Earnest Will escort missions between July 1987 and December 1988. The escorts consisted of frigates, missile cruisers, battleships, amphibious ships, destroyers, and minesweepers. The tankers had been re-flagged with the Stars and Stripes, and the area guarded was from the Gulf of Oman to Kuwait. Aerial reconnaissance was established by P-3C Orions from Saudi Arabia as well as AWACS. E-2C Hawkeyes from an American aircraft carrier Battle Group in the Arabian Sea also flew reconnaissance missions. As an embarrassment, the first supertanker re-flagged and escorted under Operation Earnest Will was the *Bridgeton,* which struck a sea mine. The tanker made port, but the United States learned that deterrence was no substitute for action.

During the Tanker War phase of American involvement in the Persian Gulf in the 1980s, 546 ships were sunk or damaged and 430 civilian mariners were killed. Without the presence of U.S. Navy forces, the losses would have been far greater.

The Iran-Iraq War ended in 1988 by a formally signed cease-fire, and both sides had been decimated and financially strapped. Both claimed some degree of success, yet millions of people were killed with no real goal being achieved. Two years later, another war was about to begin when Iraq decided to invade Kuwait.

THE INVASION OF KUWAIT

Kuwait had been separate from the Basra Province of the old Ottoman Empire (now, the Basra Governorate of Iraq) for nearly a century, despite the challenges from Baghdad. Discussions between the Kuwaiti and Iraqi governments had been ongoing even up to July 1990. However, Kuwait was not going to agree to come under the rule of Saddam Hussein. Accordingly, Iraqi ground forces invaded Kuwait with overwhelming force on August 2, 1990, in spite of the concerns the American ambassador stated to Iraq about troop concentrations on the Kuwaiti border. Saddam Hussein had the impression that his conquest of Kuwait would cause a rebuke from certain nations, but he was certain that mounting any campaign to eject his forces would not be worth the effort and cost. He was wrong and completely misinterpreted the will of the United Nations and the United States.

From August 8, 1990, until January 17, 1991, the United States and a coalition of thirty-five nations built up a force of six aircraft carrier battle groups, two surface-action groups, scores of other warships, 2,430 fixed-wing aircraft, and over 500,000 combat-ready soldiers or marines. They were poised to do battle with Iraq's Republican Guard and the rest of its ground forces, comprising 1.2 million men, 5,800 tanks, 3,850 artillery pieces, a Soviet-designed air-defense system that was the envy of the region, and an air force of 750 fighter aircraft and 200 other planes. On January 17, 1991, the coalition, satisfied with its force disposition and ability to defeat Saddam's armed forces, launched the attack from the air, sea, and then the ground.

THE U.S. NAVY, USS MISSOURI, AND DESERT STORM

There was some question as to whether the battleships would be part of Desert Storm. The USS *Iowa* was no longer considered to be a fleet asset because of the tragic flare-back and explosion in the number-two turret in 1989. Also, the USS *New Jersey* was slated for decommissioning, as were the *Missouri* and *Wisconsin.* However, it was decided to deploy the *Missouri* and the *Wisconsin* with a battle group to the Persian Gulf after all.

Actually, soon after Saddam Hussein invaded Kuwait, the *Missouri* was spared for further service.

During the early hours of the morning, the *Missouri* fires at Iraqi military targets in Kuwait. The Iraqi Army had never seen such power and destructiveness dealt out by a warship and was not likely to forget as the high-explosive rounds exploded near or on the targets. The *Missouri* and sister USS *Wisconsin* fired well over a thousand 16-inch shells during the Persian Gulf War, and most to good effect. *U.S. Navy*

Over the bow of the battleship, the main battery's turret two fires at a target called in on Kuwaiti soil, to destroy Iraqi troops and artillery emplacements. A few 16-inch shells were far more economical than a Tomahawk missile for such a fire mission. The explosion outside the barrel lights up the entire area around the bow. *U.S. Navy*

She was placed on twenty-four-hour standby for transit to the war zone. The ship had to be resupplied, and the possibility of chemical weapons ensured that the crew was trained to deal with this contingency. Additionally, the 1989 explosion on the *Iowa* still was foremost on many minds, so additional training was provided in main-battery gunnery, and the powder bags were restocked with new and improved charges.

The *Missouri* also picked up two additional units of personnel who were brand-new to battleship life. The scout aircraft of World War II had given way to the helicopter, and now remote-control aircraft would be their eyes. A group of RPV, or remotely piloted vehicles, were brought aboard with a detachment of twenty-two technicians to operate the fourteen-foot-long, four-hundred-pound aircraft. They were controlled by the trained personnel aboard the ship and launched by rocket in order to get them to 70 knots. After scouting ahead or reporting battle damage, they could be recalled and then trapped astern in a huge volleyball-like net. With its television camera, the RPV could send back images of anything the operator wanted to see and record.

The *Missouri* also picked up a detachment of explosive ordnance disposal (EOD) specialists to deal with one of the Gulf's primary threats, sea mines. The team of five would dispose of floating mines when they were discovered. The *Missouri* passed through the Strait of Hormuz on January 3, 1991, and six days later the EOD team blew up a mine that had been discovered near the ship by the helicopter from the USS *Curts* (FFG-38). They were in the war zone for less than a week, and the EOD swimmers were veterans.

On January 17, 1991, just after midnight, the *Missouri*'s commanding officer, Capt. Albert Kaiss, notified the crew that in ten minutes they would be going to battle stations, and to take care of any of nature's calls. The *Missouri* had a strike order, and was about launch Tomahawk missiles within the next sixty minutes. At 0140, an armored launch box was opened, and a Tomahawk emerged on its way to a target in Baghdad. Next, one of the escorts fired a missile straight up using a VLS cell, and then it seemed as if the entire sky around the battleship was lit up. Six Tomahawks came out of their armored boxes and flew toward enemy targets. The *Missouri* was at war, but in

a new type of war. Its targets were over the horizon. The next order of business was to secure, and the crew went to breakfast, as no retaliation was expected from the Iraqis.

On January 18, in the darkness of night, the *Missouri* launched an additional thirteen Tomahawk missiles. One missile failed, and its backup was safely on its way forty-five minutes later. The *Missouri* successfully completed the mission for January 18, and by January 20, the ship had loosed three more missiles, for a total of twenty since the barrage began.

The nightly attacks ended for a short period, and the staff concentrated on mission planning. Of course, this was until the events surrounding Khafji, a small deserted town on very northern edge of Saudi Arabia. The Iraqi Army had secured the area and moved in troops and heavy weapons. As the *Wisconsin* was now the Tomahawk coordinator, it fell to the *Missouri* to take over fire-support coordination, and also to help level areas like Khafji, where Iraqi forces had congregated and might prove a problem for the Coalition ground troops.

In order to get close enough to the target area, the battleship had to move into dangerously shallow waters, with as little as three feet of clearance beneath the keel. On February 3, 1991, the *Missouri* fired her 16-inch rifles in anger. The last time had been against North Korean targets on March 25, 1953, or nearly thirty-eight years before!

The first targets were hardened concrete command-and-control bunkers. In the nights that followed, the ships blasted one target after another, and during one shoot, the fire-control team used the RPV and its infrared sensing system to send back high-definition images. The aircraft, flying between 1,500 and 2,000 feet, spotted a truck making short stops, with the driver getting out and delivering something as soldiers ran out to pick up his delivery. It was surmised that this was the chow truck, and all of its stops were plotted. On February 4, the *Missouri* demolished all of the stops made by the truck, and destroyed countless pieces of equipment and scores of soldiers.

On February 5, the *Missouri* fired 112 16-inch shells at artillery positions, and destroyed all of them plus support vehicles. A week later, the *Missouri* was back firing at Khafji and lobbed sixty rounds from her main battery. The sea mine problem was still with the

A daytime shoot of the two forward main-battery turrets. After the shells have left the barrel, a strong blast of air ejects any possible burning residue in the barrel. This prevents a premature explosion or a fire in the turret. *U.S. Navy*

fleet assembled in the Persian Gulf off Kuwait, and the USS *Tripoli* (LPH-10) and the cruiser USS *Princeton* (CG-59) struck mines that put them out of the war.

It was not long before the U.S. Navy and Marine Corps initiated a major feint against the Iraqi forces in Kuwait. The Republican Guard knew that the Coalition would be attacking from either Saudi Arabia or the sea. The navy and marines began the feint as early as February 23, 1991, when the *Missouri* came in close to Kuwait, as if to soften the beach defenses in preparation for an invasion. Of course, there was still

the mine problem, and it was necessary to clear an area for the ship to close the beach for its fire-support mission. Ultimately, the EOD team cleared ten mines and disposed of them, so the team was a valuable addition to the ship's crew.

The first target was Faylakah Island, and on February 24 the *Missouri* opened fire at 2315. The results were spectacular, and the Iraqis were next observed moving in excessive forces and heavy artillery to repel a landing. The following day at 0300 hours, the battleship again opened fire on the beaches and in

The *Missouri* can now safely enter a harbor in the Persian Gulf without fear of Iraqi response or mines. The war came to a swift end, due the rapidity of the Coalition forces outflanking and outsmarting the Iraqi leadership. The Persian Gulf War of 1990–91 was one of the shortest in history. The Coalition lost under four hundred personnel, whereas the Iraqi armed forces lost anywhere from one hundred thousand to two hundred thousand. Technology played an immense part in this victory. *U.S. Navy*

a two-hour period fired 133 rounds. All in all, the plan was working very well, except that the Iraqi forces also moved in Silkworm missile defenses. Suddenly, a missile was inbound, and virtually everyone in the fleet gathered near the beaches recognized the threat, especially those aboard the *Missouri*. There were chaff systems going off from a number of ships, and then the Royal Navy destroyer HMS *Gloucester* fired two antiaircraft Sea Dart missiles at the Silkworm. One missed, and the other blew it out of the sky. The threat was over. Later, another Silkworm battery was discovered some twenty miles inland, and the ship's RPV sent back images. The *Missouri* fired fifty rounds of 16-inch shells and obliterated the target.

During the shore bombardment, the *Missouri* fired 289 rounds of 16-inch shells from its main battery, and successfully helped to fool the Iraqi forces as to the intentions of the Coalition. By February 27, the old battleship had fired some 611 rounds as part of the false invasion plan, and overall, during its deployment, its main battery fired 759 rounds with great effect.

The land war was over on February 28, with a complete victory for the Coalition. The much feared Republican Guard ran out of Kuwait, stealing everything they could, yet many died on the "highway of death" in the vehicles they used to escape in. Coalition aircraft caught them on the ground and decimated the escaping Iraqi army. The *Missouri* and its sister, the *Wisconsin*, contributed in no small part to the overall victory. It was the perfect swan song for the battleship.

The ship remained in the Gulf until March 21, 1991, and then moved through the Strait of Hormuz and homeward. There were stopovers at Sydney, Australia, and Pearl Harbor. The voyage from Pearl Harbor to the *Missouri*'s home port of Long Beach, California, was bittersweet, as it was a "tiger cruise,"

in which relatives of the crew are allowed to make the final trip. As an added bonus, the ship demonstrated all of its weapons, including salvoes from the 16-inch main battery. This was the last time in history that a battleship fired its main battery, and it was witnessed by the crew and many of their families.

The *Missouri* steamed into Long Beach on May 13, 1991, exactly six months to the day that she left to go to war. The greeting was something to behold, and there was one final duty for the battleship: to visit Pearl Harbor on December 7, 1991, for the fiftieth anniversary of the Japanese attack. President George Bush and First Lady Barbara Bush would be on hand for the ceremony. The crew really worked hard to prepare the ship for this final honor. The *Missouri* had again triumphed in war and made the nation proud.

The *Missouri* has made its transit back to its home port of Long Beach, California, and thousands of well-wishers and tourists have come to see this famous ship. Next stop after cleaning and repainting would be Pearl Harbor for the December 7, 1991, fiftieth anniversary of the Japanese attack on Pearl Harbor. *U.S. Navy*

On March 31, 1992, the USS *Missouri* was moored against Pier Echo in the Long Beach Naval Shipyard. After the speeches, the American flag was hauled down, and the *Missouri* was decommissioned for the last time. There were few dry eyes in the audience as they watched an era come to an end. It had begun near the turn of the century and lasted a mere one hundred years before the last battleship was retired. It was too expensive to maintain the ship, and the Soviet threat had evaporated with the collapse of their government. Next stop was the Inactive Ship Maintenance Facility in Bremerton, Washington, and into mothballs again. The only way the ship could come alive again was to become a museum. *U.S. Navy*

The *Missouri* is carefully warped alongside a pier on Battleship Row, some five hundred yards aft of the USS *Arizona* Memorial. This image clearly shows the weathering of the ship's decks and upper works. Sun and saltwater are the greatest enemies of steel ships. It will not be too long before she is in shipshape and Bristol fashion. *U.S. Navy*

CHAPTER EIGHT

THE USS MISSOURI MUSEUM

THE EXCITEMENT AND GLORY OF BEING AT the fiftieth anniversary of the attack on Pearl Harbor began to wane as the ship steered down the channel leading out of Pearl Harbor and back to its home port of Long Beach. Soon, the flag was hauled down on March 31, 1992, and the *Missouri* joined the ranks of hundreds of famous, not famous, and nondescript warships that had been retired. Her next stop was Bremerton, Washington, for inactivation. There she was stricken from the Naval Vessel Register (NVR) and now could scrapped, used as a target for modern warships, or donated as a museum ship to some lucky city or entity.

Yet, the *Missouri* was and is probably the most popular and famous ship in the U.S. Navy, aside from the USS *Constitution*, which is still a commissioned ship. Therefore, the fight to secure the *Missouri* as a museum ship began as soon as she was made available for donation or other possibilities. The ideas of scrapping this great ship, using her as a target, or sinking her to form an artificial fish reef were considered abhorrent. Consequently, organizations in Bremerton, San Francisco, and Hawaii all put in bids for the ship to be a museum piece in their area.

After a spirited competition, Secretary of the Navy John H. Dalton approved the plan put forth by the USS *Missouri* Memorial Association of Honolulu, Hawaii. The people in San Francisco were very disappointed,

The port side of the *Missouri*'s bridge, depicting all of the combat ribbons and stars for service aboard. To the far right are ten Iraqi mines that were destroyed by the ship's EOD team in the Persian Gulf. The ship has now been repainted and looks almost factory fresh. *U.S. Navy*

and have now worked quite diligently to acquire the USS *Iowa*, which is currently in the Suisun Bay Reserve Fleet in Benicia, California.

The contract to transfer the *Missouri* from the U.S. Navy to the Memorial Association of Honolulu took place on May 4, 1998, six years after the ship had been decommissioned. During the years the ship was moored in Bremerton, there was sufficient time for various barnacles and sea growth to attach themselves to the hull. It would be an impossible situation for the ship to bring this kind of underwater growth to Pearl Harbor, because it had been determined that the growth would damage the ecosystem of the harbor. Consequently, an innovative idea solved the problem.

RIGHT The *Missouri* sits serenely at its mooring along Battleship Row, long after being refurbished. As a museum ship, there are none better, and this particular view shows the great ship to its best advantage. USS Missouri *Memorial Association*

In 2005, billboards depicting the victorious Russian military were placed in at least twenty locations in Moscow. In a terrible embarrassment to the Russian government, the artists were convinced that the *Missouri* was a unit in the Russian Navy. The Russian president was beside himself with fury, and had the billboards all removed. It is unknown as to the fate of the artists. *U.S. Navy*

LEFT This spectacular view of the two forward turrets of the *Missouri*'s main battery, with the USS *Arizona* Memorial just over the bow, was captured in March 2006. *Author's collection*

BOTTOM Veterans of the USS *Missouri* pose on her deck after a recent anniversary of the end of World War II. The men have served aboard the ship from World War II and Korea to the Persian Gulf. There are many ceremonies held aboard the ship because of its historic value and aesthetic beauty. *U.S. Navy*

The *Missouri* rests in her final place of honor next to Ford Island in Pearl Harbor. The photograph was taken in 2006 from the same height as the attacking Japanese torpedo planes first came over Ford Island on the morning of December 7, 1941. *Author's collection*

On May 23, 1998, the *Missouri* was towed down to the Columbia River, across the bar, and into Astoria, Oregon's, harbor. There the ship sat for two weeks, and the sea growth acquired in Bremerton was destroyed by the fresh water of the Columbia River.

After the ship was pronounced safe for the fragile waters of Pearl Harbor, she was hooked onto a seagoing tug, and on June 22, the battleship arrived off Diamond Head and was escorted into Pearl Harbor by the U.S. Coast Guard and scores of small craft. A mooring had been specifically chosen for the great ship, and it was to honor the other battleship in harbor, the USS *Arizona* (BB-39).

The *Missouri* was to act as a bookend for the war in the Pacific. The USS *Arizona* Memorial would signify the onset of war, and the *Missouri*, victory in the Pacific War. However, the *Missouri* was not to take anything from the *Arizona* Memorial or the more than one thousand men who were entombed in the ship. The *Missouri* was tied up to a mooring five hundred yards from the *Arizona* Memorial. The ship was also angled in such a way that any ceremonies on the stern or fantail of the *Missouri* would be out of sight of the *Arizona* Memorial. The *Missouri*'s bow faced the USS *Arizona* as a protector of the remains of all those that have been interred aboard the memorial. All of the plans for placing the *Missouri* were designed to show absolute respect and in no way eclipse the importance and sacred value of the USS *Arizona* Memorial.

Hundreds of volunteers crawled all over the *Missouri* to make it into the best battleship museum in the United States. Thousands of gallons of gray paint were slapped on, and an entire team of specialists took over responsibility for polishing and repairing the teakwood decks. The interior was cleaned and those areas that could be open to the public were brought back to their original condition. All of the work paid off on January 29, 1999, when the USS *Missouri* Memorial Association of Honolulu, Hawaii, opened the showpiece battleship museum to the public. Since that time, hundreds of thousands of tourists have come from all over the world to tread its decks and look through the ship's compartments. A special treat is to stand near the spot where the Japanese surrendered in 1945, thus formally ending World War II.

Today, the ship is run like a well-oiled machine, with over 2,500 permanent volunteers that are organized to maintain the ship in pristine condition. Truly, the *Missouri* is the most respected battleship in the world.

BIBLIOGRAPHY

PRIMARY MATERIALS

Private Papers: Manuscript/Photo Files

Arnold, Bruce Makoto. Photo collection.

Bonner, Carolyn E. Private papers and photos.

Bonner, Kermit H. Private papers and photo collection.

Bonner, Kermit H., Sr. Private papers and photo collection.

Archival Collections:
Manuscripts/Photo Collections

Call Bulletin newspaper file, Treasure Island Museum.

Department of Defense, naval files.

Treasure Island Museum photo files.

United States Naval Institute.

United States Navy, Office of Information.

USS *Missouri* Memorial.

Interviews

Burgess, Rick. Managing Editor, *Sea Power,* Navy League, various issues, 2003–2006.

Commander Surface Force, Pearl Harbor, March 2006.

Public Affairs Office, Kitsap Naval Station, August 2004

Tauyan, Agnes. Deputy Director, Public Affairs, Naval Station, Pearl Harbor.

SECONDARY MATERIALS

Books

A Day in the Life of the Soviet Union. Collins Publishers, Inc., 1987.

Blackman, Paul. *The World's Warships.* Hanover House, 1960.

Blackman, Raymond V. B. *Jane's Fighting Ships 1968–1969.* BPC Publishing, Ltd., 1969.

Bonds, Ray, editor. *Russian Military Power.* Bonanza Books, 1982.

Bonner, Kit. "Final Voyages", Turner Publishing, 1996.

———. *Cold War at Sea.* Motor Books International, 2000.

———. *Great Naval Disasters.* Motor Books International, 1998.

———. *USS Iowa at War.* Zenith Press, 2007.

Dictionary of American Naval Fighting Ships. U.S. Government Printing Office, 1979.

Friedman, Norman. "U.S. Cruisers", Naval Institute Press, 1984.

———. *U.S. Destroyers.* Naval Institute Press, 1982.

———. *U.S. Small Combatants.* Naval Institute Press, 1987.

Faulkner, Keith. *Jane's Warship Recognition Guide.* Harper Collins, 1996. *Jane's Fighting Ships.* Various volumes,1944–97.

Jordan, John. *Modern U.S. Navy.* Prentice Hall, 1986.

Jentschura, Hansgeorg, Peter Mickel, and Dieter Jung. *Warships of the Imperial Japanese Navy, 1869–1945.* Naval Institute Press, 1977.

Karnow, Stanley. *Vietnam, A History.* The Viking Press, 1983.

Miller, David. *The Cold War, A Military History.* John Murray Publishing, 1998.

Moore, Capt. John E. *The Soviet Navy Today.* Stein and Day, 1975.

Moore, Capt. John, R.N. *Jane's American Fighting Ships of the 20th Century.* Mallard Press, 1991.

Morison, Samuel Eliot. *History of the United States Naval Operations in World War II.* Atlantic-Little Brown, 1962.

Muir, Malcolm, Jr. *Black Shoes and Blue Water.* U.S. Government Printing Office, 1996.

Preston, Anthony. *Warships of the World.* Jane's, 1980.

Scott, Harriet, and William F. Scott. *The Armed Forces of the USSR.* Westview Press, 1979.

Sea Power Almanac. NLUS, 1991–2006.

Silverstone, Paul. *U.S. Navy 1945 to the Present.* Arms and Armour Press, 1991.

———. *U.S. Warships Since 1945.* Naval Institute Press, 1987.

Sommervile, Donald. *World War II Day by Day.* Dorset Press, 1989.

Stillwell, Paul. *Battleship Missouri, An Illustrated History.* Naval Institute Press, 1996.

Sultzberger, C. L. *The American Heritage Picture History of World War IIB.* Crown Publishers, 1966.

Sweetman, Jack. *American Naval History.* Naval Institute Press, 1984.

Walker, Martin. *The Cold War.* Owl Books, 1993.

Wertheim, Eric. *Combat Fleets of the World.* Naval Institute Press, 2005.

Winton, John. *The War at Sea: 1939 through 1945.* Pimlico, 1967.

Articles and Essays

All Hands. Bureau of Naval Personnel. November 1945.

Atkinson, James D., and Yeuell, Donovan P. "Must We Have World War III?" *Naval Institute Proceedings,* July 1956.

Beers, Henry P. "American Naval Detachment, Turkey, 1919–1924", *Warship International* 13, No. 3, 1976.

Bonner, Kit. "Tonkin Gulf Incident." *Sea Classics,* 1996.

"The Cold War." Grolier Electronic Encyclopedia, 1993.

Eller, Rear Adm. E. M. "Soviet Bid for the Sea." *Naval Institute Proceedings,* June 1955.

Finney, John W. "Soviets Imperil U.S. Ships." *Naval Institute Proceedings,* June 1965 (article reprinted from the *New York Times,* April 4, 1965).

Matloff, Maurice. "The Soviet Union and the War in the West." *Naval Institute Proceedings,* March, 1956.

Meister, Jurg. "The Soviet Navy in World War II." *Naval Institute Proceedings,* August 1957.

Sea Classics. Various issues, 2000–2006.

Sea Power. Issues, 1991, 1997.

Storia Militare. Various issues, 2004–2006.

Surface Warfare. Various issues, 2003–2007.

"U.S. Naval Battle Force Changes, January–December 1997." *Naval Institute Proceedings,* May 1998.

Warships International, Fleet Review. Various issues, 2005–2007.

Watt, Donald C. "Stalin's First Bid for Sea Power, 1933–1939." *Naval Institute Proceedings,* June 1964.

Webber, Mark, Lt., USN. "*Kashin*-Class Missile Frigates." *Naval Institute Proceedings,* June 1965.

Winnefeld, James. "The Cold War Power Spectrum." *Naval Institute Proceedings,* January 1960.

Websites

Naval Vessel Register: http://www.nvr.navy.mil/
Royal Navy: http://www.royal-navy.mod.uk/
Russian Navy: www.navy.ru/main-e.htm
U.S. Navy: http://www.navy.mil
U.S. Coast Guard: http://www.uscg.mil
Wikipedia: http://wikipedia.org

INDEX

Other **Zenith Press** titles of interest:

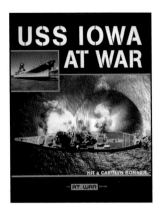

USS IOWA AT WAR
ISBN 978-0-7603-2804-0

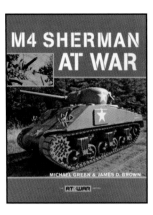

M4 SHERMAN AT WAR
ISBN 978-0-7603-2784-5

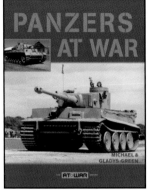

PANZERS AT WAR
ISBN 978-0-7603-2152-2

NAVY
ISBN 978-0-7603-2972-6

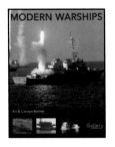

MODERN WARSHIPS
ISBN 978-0-7603-2950-4

NORMANDY
ISBN 978-0-7603-3327-3

ZENITH
PRESS

Find us on the internet at
www.ZenithPress.com

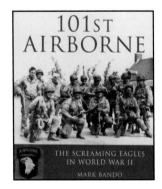

101ST AIRBORNE
ISBN 978-0-7603-2984-9

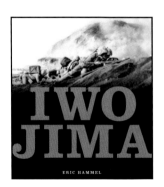

IWO JIMA
ISBN 978-0-7603-2520-9

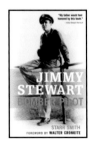

JIMMY STEWART
ISBN 978-0-7603-2199-7